T0384214

Freedom within a Framework

Freedom within a Framework
Hearing the Voice of the Customer on the Factory Floor

Paul G. Cafaro

Routledge
Taylor & Francis Group

A PRODUCTIVITY PRESS BOOK

First published 2020
by Routledge
52 Vanderbilt Avenue, New York, NY 10017

and by Routledge
2 Park Square, Milton Park, Abingdon, Oxon, OX14 4RN

Routledge is an imprint of the Taylor & Francis Group, an informa business

ISBN: 978-0-367-08577-3 (hbk)
ISBN: 978-0-429-02311-8 (ebk)

Typeset in Minion
by codeMantra

Artwork and figures designed by Lewis E. Cafaro

This book was not a single person effort. As the saying goes, it takes two to tango. I am very blessed to have my wife, Donna, as my partner. She spent countless hours refining my manuscripts and making this book possible.

Contents

PART 2   Design and R&D Viewpoint

Author

Paul G. Cafaro is the Global R&D Director of Strategic Continuous Improvement for the Sherwin-Williams Company. He is responsible for achieving world-class innovation excellence by bridging the commercial needs of the business and customer's end use. Prior to joining Sherwin-Williams, Paul held several operations and leadership positions with increasing responsibility for Dow Chemical Company and Tyco International.

Paul earned his Chemical Engineering degree from Illinois Institute of Technology in Chicago, IL, and has completed post-graduate studies at University of Wisconsin, Madison, and Massachusetts Institute of Technology. Additionally, Paul is a Certified Master Black Belt and has been invited to speak at several international conferences and manufacturing summits.

Introduction

We all have been there. The frustrating feeling of not being understood. It can test our patience, wreck our relationships, and for a company, it could mean losing customers. This book is about how to listen to the customer's voice, not just those in the customer service department but everybody, right down to the factory floor. When a business can align its people to know and understand what their buyers are saying, then that company becomes like a collimated laser beam, quickly addressing the problems, delivering products (or services) that not only satisfy the customers but wows them.

Customers ask something about our product and many times it may sound easy and straightforward just to know later that it is not what the customer really wanted. The Voice of the Customer is often elusive, so we will help you understand your customer's voice, translating their words into the products that we deliver to them.

Each part of the book places emphasis on three specific business functions, and they will be interconnected in the last part when we put it all together. The three business functions that need to work as one cohesive and unified team are: commercial (sales and marketing), research and development (product properties and services), and operations or manufacturing (product quality). Additionally, each chapter explains the information in a logical and sequential manner, so the reader can thread the knowledge imparted in one section of the book to the next. It is advisable to read the book sequentially, and if you are keen to know more about a topic, you can use the table of contents or index to focus on a specific subject.

OVERVIEW AND HOW THIS BOOK CAN HELP YOU

The key to an effective relationship with your customer is to clearly articulate their needs and wants by fully understanding their viewpoint. This is easier said than done. Companies that offer superior products not only deliver outstanding quality and services but also complement it by listening to the Voice of the Customer, the "VOC". The VOC involves active listening of your client's requirements, resonating throughout your organization all the way to the factory floor, becoming the paramount goal.

Listening to the customer describe the pros and cons of our product clarifies what they desire, by capturing everything they said may give us as suppliers a view of being complete and full understanding of their viewpoints. On the other hand, capturing their input verbatim is not enough because the content needs to be interpreted. Once the customer's voice has been defined, it can be threaded within the framework of the supplier's business functions throughout the entire organization, having a direct impact on the client's experience. Achieving this connectivity creates an enterprise capable of turning out outstanding products that surprise and delight the customer.

The skill to transform their needs into practical solutions will be explored in this book. We will explain how to obtain this goal and harmonize different business departments to address the customer's needs: these broader business functions include commercial, research and development, and operations. The framework of the Houses of Quality will be our main tool. We will navigate through the houses and accumulate the details needed to ensure a clear and quantitative view of the customer and each business function. Several tools will augment the Houses of Quality such as the Kano model, brainstorming, Pareto analysis, and a few others. Also, depending on the complexity of the product being made, it will determine the number of houses needed. The approaches taken throughout these pages will highlight the structure needed for success and how to make a product with the customer in mind.

Take the journey through these pages to explore your company through a different lens, so you, the strategist, can map the customer's voice all the way to the factory floor.

Part 1

Commercial Viewpoint

1

Understand the Voice of the Customer

1.1 FREEDOM WITHIN A FRAMEWORK

You are embarking on a journey of discovery. This event will lead to a greater understanding of the voice of your customer. We will take this voyage of exploration using a supporting mechanism, a framework that will be a roadmap of your business' success. But first you need to accept the idea of going slow to go fast. Let me repeat that, you need to go slow to go fast! Sounds contradictory? Let me expand on it.

Study the chart in Figure 1.1 and note its complexity. Now look at the second flowchart (Figure 1.2). At first glance, which flowchart seems more complicated, the first or the second one?

How did you come to that choice? Complexity, if interpreted as number of steps, may make the first flowchart seem complex. In a different manner, complexity defined as reaching a desired option, either option 1 or 2, makes the second flowchart complex. Why is that? The initial glance of the second flowchart seems simpler; however, it has many undefined paths

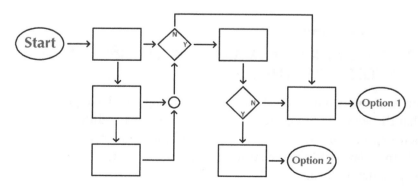

FIGURE 1.1
The first flowchart.

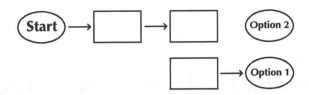

FIGURE 1.2
The second flowchart.

to get to option 1 or 2. The steps are not connected, left to interpretation, using assumptions on how to leap from one step to the next; this chart is the more complicated one, as it has no framework.

These flowchart analogies are akin to a travel app with a detailed map which can be used to plan a road trip. The map outlines all possible road types to connect point A to B, highways, small paved roads, gravel roads, off road, etc. By taking the time to study the map ahead of the trip, it can save you valuable time later. Right there you are going slow to go fast! You are learning about your journey and experiences ahead of time, so when you are in your trip, you can fully enjoy the time you invested in it.

The same commitment needs to be done to understand your customer. Together, we will take time to understand them, and during that process, we will use a framework to build the houses of quality like a roadmap of success. Once the houses are built and linked, it will allow us to zip through these like the connected boxes in Figure 1.1. Now that we are learning how to go slow to go fast, let us start understanding our most important person in our endeavor: our customer.

1.2 CUSTOMER WANTS AND CUSTOMER NEEDS: WHY THE GAP?

Our customers have expectations. We, as suppliers, have perceptions of what those expectations are. The gap is defined as the difference between their expectations and our perceptions. Aligning them will enhance not only the relationship of the customer and us as suppliers but also improve the product performance.

The Voice of the Customer (VOC) articulates directly what they desire and what they need. Our understanding of their needs and wants can be elusive. We feel at times that we are navigating through an arduous and sinuous path; however, we are not sure if we achieved the full comprehension of the VOC. If the customer says, "I like the high quality of your product," do you clearly know what they mean by quality? Let's explore the key words *high quality*. You may have a definition for it and they may have another. Notice that *high quality* could be interpreted in multiple ways. Sometimes to get the right definition of that product property may seem more artistic than scientific. Confusion may occur because assumptions are used as facts. One way to overcome this misunderstanding is to define the product with its properties or attributes, determining those as either facts or assumptions. We will show this process in detail with copious examples throughout this book.

How do we know if we are using assumptions? How do we discern our version of *high quality* from our customer's version of *high quality*? First, we need to identify if our definition, as a producer, is clearly outlined and articulated. Second, we examine how our customer's definition, as a user, defines *high quality* of our product. Having these two responses, do they compare or do they contrast each other. If they match, the definition shows alignment, but let's not make a victory lap yet. We both have agreed on that attribute of *high quality*. Now validation needs to be made with all key attributes of our product to ensure that there is 100% agreement since it is common to see misalignment of product properties between the supplier and the customer.

A way to mitigate the risk of misalignment involves learning about their wants and needs. Let's say we make coatings, and the customer makes plastic tubes which uses our bright colored finish. The tube is designed to be bent and the coating should be flexible enough to withstand the bending without peeling or cracking the colorful finish. When we make the coating, *high quality* to us is a painted surface that doesn't crack at a 90° bend. We also want to match their desired color with a reflectiveness at 85% gloss level. As a supplier, we did a tremendous amount of research and development to make a product that meets those demanding specifications. On the other hand, the customer's definition of *high quality* was something entirely different. When we interviewed the customer and asked them to define what good tubing is, they considered other parameters we didn't think about, such as coating smoothness, consistent thickness, and fast production rate. Gloss, cracking, and color match were not even in their mind! Our company placed so much time and costs developing these specifications we thought were important.

We need to ask ourselves whose expectations are being met. How can this definition of the VOC be so disconnected between what they expect and what we perceived? This misalignment happens because we didn't dig deep enough and truly translate the VOC; instead, we made assumptions of what we think they need. Capturing their voice with the actual specification variables of the product and joining them together will be a first step to clarify and augment what was missing from our original assumptions. This concept may sound trivial or basic, but it is a fundamental issue for the success in providing a product to the customer that they will be delighted to have.

Let me illustrate this idea with another example that all of us are familiar with. If you go to a high-end coffee shop for a premium priced cup of espresso coffee which is approximately twice the price of what you would pay at another shop, what commands the premium price? If you conduct an informal survey as you walk around the shop, some of the replies you may hear: "I really like these comfortable chairs with the free Wi-Fi access." or "I like sitting here by the window, looking outside, seeing the city and the people going by." or "I like the calm music and clean bathrooms." You will find that none of them said they want their coffee hot in clean cups. Why does that matter? That will be the equivalent of asking our plastic tube customer that the painted product shouldn't peel off. Those product attributes are called the must-be or basic characteristics inherent in the product. They should not be spelled out, they are understood. The point is that our customer has needs and wants that are spoken and unspoken; in the next few chapters, we will outline how to capture and capitalize on those customer requirements.

A conversation with the customer needs to take place to gather all the facts around the product you provide them and how they use it in their manufacturing process. In other words, how does your product fit as an integral part of the whole. In order to gather what your customer expects, it is best to do it face to face. Prior to this visit, make a list of key questions that will be used.

The key questions are developed with the input from the commercial team, Figure 1.3. One of the individuals that will help craft those questions could be the marketing manager. The marketing manager plays a critical role to understand the positioning of your product in the market, phrasing the right questions that will be asked to the customer. Another group from the commercial function that needs to be involved in gathering the VOC is the sales department.

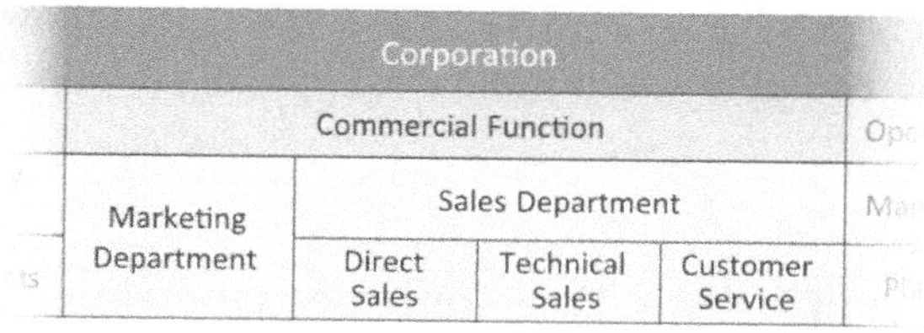

Corporation				
Commercial Function				Op...
Marketing Department	Sales Department			M...
	Direct Sales	Technical Sales	Customer Service	P...

FIGURE 1.3
The commercial function.

The sales department has three different sub-functions: direct sales, technical sales, and customer service. Let's expand on the differences between direct sales and technical sales. Direct sales team members are involved in cultivating a relationship with the customer from a price and product satisfaction standpoint and interacts with the customer often. They will dictate a price that is based on certain factors the customer is willing to pay. Technical sales typically verify that your product's performance is working as designed at the customer's facility and specifications are met. The two are integral for the total success and satisfaction at the customer's processes. Direct sales and technical sales have a constant dialog with our client related to the application of our product at their plant. On the other hand, our customer service department receives requests from our client; it is typically a one-way communication. Seldom will a customer service representative reach out to the client unless it is a follow-up call. Depending on how well all three commercial interactions are delivered could become a proxy on how the customer would perceive your product and even your company.

1.3 DEFINE THE QUESTIONS FOR THE VOC

Clear and concise questions are an important aspect of gathering the VOC. Having the wrong questions or the wrong sentence structure may lead to the wrong conclusions when asking customers about certain concepts or attributes of our product. In this section, we will highlight key dimensions for superior quality questions that will help extract meaningful data from your clients, but first, we must start how to structure those questions accurately. We will focus on five different dimensions that will give us a balanced view of what we're striving for; these are followed by sample questions that compare a substandard approach versus an improved format.

1.3.1 Dimension 1: Only One Topic per Question

Multiple ideas strung into one question may blur the impact of one idea or topic with the other. In doing so, the answer becomes confounded and not separated; it is best to have two separate questions to clearly understand the impact of each idea (Table 1.1).

1.3.2 Dimension 2: Avoid Asking Leading Questions Which May Force a Biased Answer

The concept of a leading question has the answer already built-in, using this type of sentence structure affirms an assumption or choice to be made. The following examples in Table 1.2 will better describe this type of question.

TABLE 1.1

Dimension 1: Only One Topic per Question

Substandard	Improved
Are you satisfied with our on-time delivery using our preferred supplier?	Are you satisfied with on-time delivery of our products?
	How would you define the quality of service from our preferred supplier?
Does the product have the correct gloss and appearance when using our coating?	Does the finished product have the correct gloss when using our coating?
	Does the finished product have the appropriate appearance when using our coating?

TABLE 1.2

Dimension 2: Avoid Asking Leading Questions Which May Force a Biased Answer

Substandard	Improved
Do you agree that our new preferred supplier is better?	How would you define the quality of service from our new preferred supplier?
How much better is the gloss from our second batch compared to the first?	Please describe the gloss from our second batch

TABLE 1.3

Dimension 3: The Customer Is Willing and Able to Fully Answer the Question Being Asked

Substandard	Improved
As a secondary supplier to your company, what percent of your current demand of clear coat do we currently provide you? (Question directed to finance or purchasing unfortunately neither one was present.)	As a secondary supplier to your company, what percent of your current demand of clear coat do we currently provide you? (Question directed to finance or purchasing. Verify that both are invited to the focus group. If one person is not present, the other one could have the same information.)
The quality specifications for gloss are set to 85% at 60°. Could we reduce these to 75% at 60°. (Question directed primarily to the quality department and that function was not represented.)	The quality specifications for gloss are set to 85% at 60°. How much lower can we reduce the gloss and still meet your satisfaction? (Question directed primarily to the quality department. A quality representative was present at the meeting; in addition, the manufacturing manager was able to provide a unique perspective.)

1.3.3 Dimension 3: Customer Is Willing and Able to Fully Answer the Question Being Asked

It is important that the questions are directed to the individuals that can provide us the answers we are seeking. Instead of using a survey with our customer, we will use the focus group interview approach. We need to carefully select those individuals that will participate, so we will be able to collect complete information of our questions (Table 1.3).

1.3.4 Dimension 4: Verify that All People that Administer the Question Interpret It the Same Way

Ensure that the wording of the question is such that it could only have one interpretation. Make sure that ambiguous meanings are minimized or eliminated when wording the questions. If new terms are used, have the interviewing team define these words or concepts ahead of time (Table 1.4).

1.3.5 Dimension 5: Verify that All Respondents Interpret the Question the Same Way

We need to stress-test these questions to ensure clarity and accuracy from a customer's perspective. It will be best to pilot these questions with your colleagues. To get honest feedback, perhaps, it would be better to set it up

TABLE 1.4

Dimension 4: Verify that All People that Administer the Question Interpret It the Same Way

Substandard	Improved
Is our new product, Model-123, viewed as high quality by your quality department?	Is our new product, Model-123, exceeding your specifications for application time as requested? In addition, how is Model-123 performing for drying time? Does the product have *low gloss* and *low odor*? or Does the product have *low gloss* and *high odor*? (Gloss and odor are paired properties. Ensure that the correct paired properties are described as intended. These properties are meaningless if they are asked separately.)

as a working lunch. A light luncheon will make the environment less formal and more of a dialog with unrestrained comments from the respondents. After all, your colleagues will have the opportunity to role-play the customer; you and your team will learn how solid your questions are with potential answers.

This chapter helped shape the questions that will be used during the focus group or interview session. In Chapter 2, we will define the close-ended questions using these rules and dimensions.

2

Kano Model: Explanation of Success (Our Business Perspective)

In this chapter, we will define step by step on how to create and make use of the Kano model. As a prerequisite, we need to define the value proposition first, putting in perspective how the customer perceives value through the product they buy from us.

2.1 DEFINE THE VALUE PROPOSITION

Value proposition is defined as the key attributes of the product and services that our customer is willing to pay. The key words here are "the customer is willing to pay." Sit back and think for a moment. Reflect on a product you currently have that is very successful. Quickly, name in your mind five key attributes that come at first glance. List these on a piece of paper. Now, let's run this scenario again, this time reflect on a product that is not doing very well. In your mind, list five key attributes that come right away. As we did before, write these below the previous list. Ask this question on each of those ten characteristics, is the customer willing to pay for it? Place a yes or no next to each property as you go down the list. Most people would find several noes and yeses when they listed all the ten product properties. If you find that your list has all affirmatives, that means the customer is willing to pay for all the attributes listed; you are one of the few that knows how to pair your product's key characteristics to your customer's needs. If you haven't matched all customer's needs, don't worry, we will go step by step to systematically extract those key attributes.

As mentioned earlier in this book, we have assumptions of which properties and attributes work for our customer. Some of these ideas are rooted with facts while others are cherished without question, having long lost their reason for their being. In addition, those suppositions may deviate our path of success, causing bias, or limiting our field of view. By taking a deeper dive and analyzing those assumptions, it will help create a clear line of sight to our value proposition.

We will expand this idea with an example that will continue throughout this book. Our hypothetical customer is called Tubing Experts who manufactures plastic tubes. Typically, these tubes are made with PVC (polyvinyl chloride) which are extruded and can be made with virgin raw materials or a mixture of recycled and virgin PVC. We are one of Tubing Experts' premier suppliers of liquid coatings. Our company, Liquid Paint Specialists, another hypothetical business, makes a paint that is applied over the plastic tube to provide the finished color and appearance that the end user will desire. The end users are typically marketing and graphic design professionals for commercial displays and exposition booths.

2.2 PRIORITIZE THE VALUE PROPOSITION

Liquid Paint Specialists would like to know more about the value proposition of the coating product that they make, capturing a list of attributes by brainstorming one or two words. They would like input from a wide viewpoint, using a multifunctional team from various areas of our business that knows about the product in question. Table 2.1 has a list of potential functions or departments that could be invited to participate. It is important to note that not all areas need to be invited. The list is intended to spark a thought, considering which functions and individuals to invite. The optimum group size to do this brainstorming exercise is between 7 and 12 people.

Now that you have assembled the individuals that will participate in this brainstorming event, you will be the facilitator by capturing single-word or two-word attributes on a flip chart or whiteboard. Encourage them to be creative, have them piggyback ideas from one another. Another option would be round-robin and keep going around until several individuals start to skip. Once they start skipping, you may have started to reach

TABLE 2.1

List of Business Functions or Departments

Customer Service	Purchasing
Distribution, logistics	Human resources
Supply chain	Manufacturing
Finance	Operations
Information technology	Marketing
Business administration	Sales
Research and development	Warehouse

the end of the brainstorming. At that point give the participants a few moments to shout out a few more ideas.

Continuing with our example company, Liquid Paint Specialists, our team of eight people have created the following list of attributes as shown in Figure 2.1.

Next step is to prioritize the list of perceived attributes using a multi-vote process. As mentioned earlier in this chapter, the key attributes of our products and services are the ones that our customer is willing to pay for. Now that we have framed that concept, put that statement on top of your flipchart or whiteboard. Use it as a focal point on how you will evaluate each one of those captured brainstormed ideas. Each participant will be given five colored stickers to place it on the attributes that they perceive "the customer is willing to pay." The rule of placing those stickers can be as follows, place a single sticker on each of those attributes that are highly important, another approach could be to place all or multiple stickers on a single attribute. You are given a limited number of votes, make

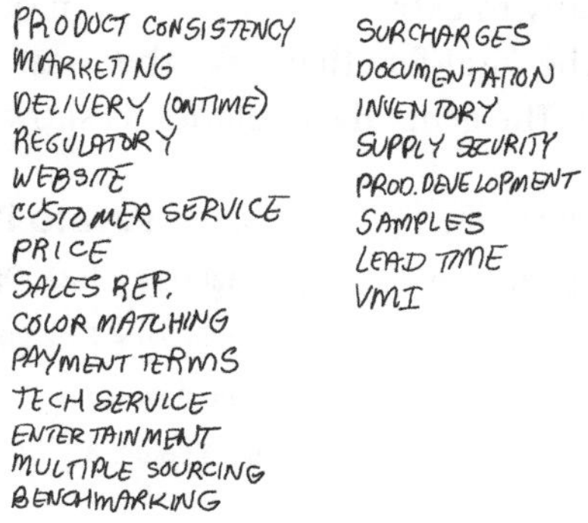

PRODUCT CONSISTENCY
MARKETING
DELIVERY (ONTIME)
REGULATORY
WEBSITE
CUSTOMER SERVICE
PRICE
SALES REP.
COLOR MATCHING
PAYMENT TERMS
TECH SERVICE
ENTERTAINMENT
MULTIPLE SOURCING
BENCHMARKING

SURCHARGES
DOCUMENTATION
INVENTORY
SUPPLY SECURITY
PROD. DEVELOPMENT
SAMPLES
LEAD TIME
VMI

FIGURE 2.1
Value proposition: list of brainstormed attributes.

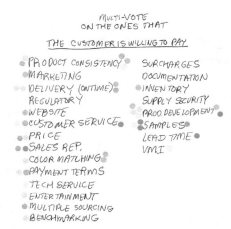

FIGURE 2.2
Value proposition: list of brainstormed attributes with voting dots.

the most of it. Figure 2.2 shows the list with voted attributes from our Liquid Paint Specialists team.

A pattern of the most wanted attributes is emerging from the original 22 brainstormed ideas. We will use the Pareto principle, the 80/20 rule, which can be interpreted as the top 20% of items having an 80% of influence. This ratio has been defined in the nineteenth century by the Italian economist and sociologist Vilfredo Pareto; he observed that 80% of the wealth in Europe was being held by 20% of the population. Another way that Pareto described this relationship is that the *vital few* or 20% have an impact over the *trivial many,* 80%. This ratio can be extrapolated into other disciplines such as engineering, healthcare, economics, sociology, and many other areas. Applying that notion to our list of attributes, we can calculate how many to extract from the list; in other words, which of these attributes are the vital few that have the most votes, being the top most influential ones. The general calculation is shown in Figure 2.3a.

(a) **Pareto Principle**

Vital Few = Total Opportunities × 20%

(b) **Pareto Principle**

Vital Few = Total Opportunities × 20%

Vital Few = 22 × 20%

Vital Few = 4.4

Vital Few ≅ 4

FIGURE 2.3
(a) Pareto principal calculation. (b) Calculate top influential items based on the Pareto principal.

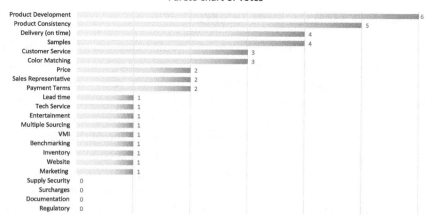

FIGURE 2.4

Value proposition: Pareto chart of voted brainstormed attributes.

Returning to our example and applying that calculation, the top 20% can be computed as shown in Figure 2.3b. We arrive to the conclusion that the top four are the most influential ones. Rounding to the nearest integer is the preferred method when the calculation leads to decimal values.

Another approximation to know if the cutoff makes sense is using a graphical approach. Look at the Pareto chart in Figure 2.4. Does the chart have a natural break? A natural break means a jump from several bars of the same value to the next group of bars, and it doesn't split the same value. In our example with four votes, it didn't split equal valued votes because we captured both attributes with the value of 4. However, if the math gave us the top five, we need to make the decision to keep one or both attributes with three votes.

Based on the calculation results, our top four are: product development, product consistency, delivery (on time), and samples. The Pareto chart, as shown in Figure 2.4, is a good visual representation to highlight those vital few top 20%.

Review these prioritized items with your brainstorming team. It is important that the pattern that emerged as the top 20% of your value proposition is discussed in detail. After each attribute has been examined, make sure you all agree to move forward with those highest voted items. These will be used to expand and craft the Kano model questions.

2.3 KANO MODEL EXPLAINED

The Kano model was introduced to the quality community in 1984 by Noriaki Kano et al. Basically, what he and the other authors saw was a limitation with quality being viewed one-dimensionally. Either you liked the product or you disliked it. It used an emotional or subjective manner of determining good versus bad. The authors expanded the concept of quality perception as a two-dimensional model. One of the dimensions was the subjective approach: how you felt about the product? The second dimension would be the objective approach: how did the product perform?

In this section, we will go step by step to understand how the Kano model structure will be used with the attributes defined for the value proposition. Figure 2.5 exemplifies the different degrees of product satisfaction using a subjective approach. The higher you move along the vertical Y axis, the happier you are with the product. The farther down you go on the axis,

FIGURE 2.5
One dimensional level of satisfaction.

you will be less satisfied with the product. Exactly in the middle of the vertical line, you will be neutral.

Adding a second dimension, a horizontal X axis, will emphasize the way the product performs based on its specifications and quality attributes as shown in Figure 2.6. Starting from the left side of the X axis, the product performs poorly. Moving to the right along the axis, the better the product performs. In the center of this line will be a neutral point of product performance.

We have a two-dimensional diagram with four different quadrants. Each quadrant has different combinations of product performance and product satisfaction. The attributes that fall in these different areas will be defined as Kano categories. These categories will be drawn with arrows crossing these different quadrants having specific meanings and interpretations of the customer's expectations and perceptions of the product performance. Kano has identified many variations of these. We will use only three.

- The first category is called the Basic Needs or Dis-satisfiers such as core, basic product properties.
- The second are Satisfiers. These are the performance attributes.
- The third Delighters! These are attributes or product needs that go beyond the customer's expectations.

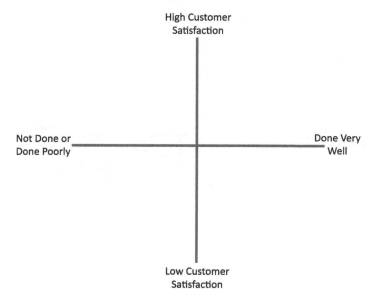

FIGURE 2.6
Two-dimensional method to measure product quality.

2.3.1 Basic Need Category

These are basic requirements or needs that are expected features or characteristic of the product. If the Basic Need is not fulfilled, the customer will be extremely dissatisfied. The Basic Need category is sometimes called Dis-satisfiers. The customer satisfaction scale for this item ranges from low customer satisfaction to neutral. The upper limit is very important to note because as we increase this Basic Need attribute, we expect customer satisfaction will increase with it; however, it can hit a limit. The highest level of fulfillment this product feature will reach is an impartial reaction. The impact of this limit could be profitable since putting more resources to improve this attribute may not translate to more satisfaction from your client. On the Kano graph, these attributes will be located on the bottom two quadrants as shown in Figure 2.7. These attributes are sometimes defined as the "price of entry" to get into the market. Most of these needs are unspoken, and they can be gathered with one-on-one interviews or focus groups. If this characteristic is missing, or it is not properly met, it will turn from an unspoken attribute to a very vocal and noticeable one. Here is an example of this type of attribute. If the car ignition does not start the vehicle, that person will be immediately disappointed; however,

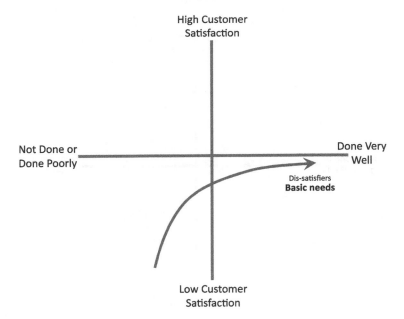

FIGURE 2.7
Kano model, Basic Needs.

if the ignition starts the car, as expected, that same person will be completely neutral about this event since that is the normal behavior. Recall the espresso coffee example being hot, does the Basic Need attribute come to mind?

2.3.2 Satisfier Category

The Satisfiers or performance needs category are product characteristics that will increase or decrease customer satisfaction by the degree that they are being fulfilled. These particular needs allow you to be competitive in the market you serve, sometimes identified as "more is better." Customers will be speaking about these types of attributes, and these are easily identified. Also, these are the ones you will see on advertisements as key features highlighting their usefulness. They can be extracted from your customers via surveys. An example of this type of category would be the enhancement of an existing feature. Using the car example from before and the specific attribute of ignition, how can we make it better? First understand how that person interacts with the ignition process. The car can be started only if the person is inside the car. Using a key to start the car is already a basic need. Now with that foundation defined, expand on that concept to make it better beyond the Basic Need. Can that person start the car being away from it? Yes, with a remote starter which is similar to an already existing feature built-in the vehicle: the remote car door entry/lock. Expanding this feature of the car ignition attribute shows an improvement on the functionality of the ignition system (moving more toward the right on the X axis) and an increase of the satisfaction level of the customer (going up on Y axis). These two dimensions of the Kano model move in tandem and migrate from being on the bottom left quadrant to the top right, as illustrated in Figure 2.8. Other examples of Satisfiers are delivery speed, delivery costs, product price, user-friendliness of the product, technical support.

2.3.3 Delighter! Category

This category of the Kano model is the most difficult one to identify; at the same time, these are counterbalanced with the most rewarding experiences that your customers will have with your product. Consider these attributes to be the ones that will give your product the extra competitive edge especially if you are first in delivering it to your customers. This innovative

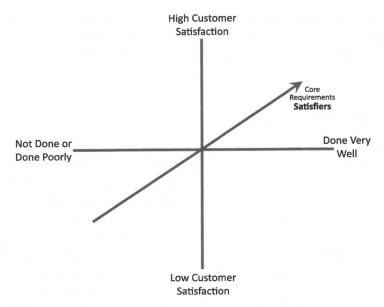

FIGURE 2.8
Kano model, Satisfiers.

attribute may exceed expectations because it is so unique; it allows you to excel in your market. Earlier, we noted that these are very difficult to identify since they are rarely spoken. The reason why it is so difficult to extract these from your customer because they are not even aware that this attribute is even available. The best way to gather these needs would be on one-on-one interviews or focus groups. A Delighter! attribute on the customer satisfaction scale ranges from neutral to high. If the Delighter! is not present in the product, the customer will not even know it is missing; therefore, they will feel neutral. On the other hand, if the customer is presented with a Delighter! attribute and sees it for the first time on the currently existing product, their satisfaction level will soar and be very excited about that added feature.

If we look at the quadrants of the Kano two-dimensional diagram, the Delighter! will be on the top left and the top right quadrants as depicted in Figure 2.9. What makes these attributes difficult to articulate is twofold: the customer often doesn't demand to have it on the product, and the business cannot easily quantify the benefit of the new unstated attribute or need. We must always ensure that the new Delighter! being offered is aligned as an added value to the business case. Remember the original definitions of the value proposition and its attributes which include

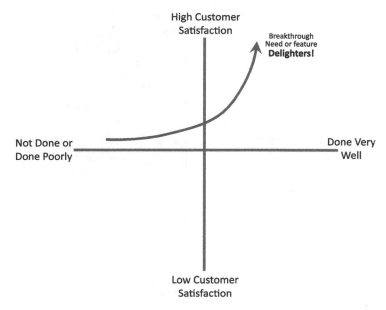

FIGURE 2.9
Kano model, Delighters!

Delighter! Is the customer willing to pay for it? Since we have used an automobile example before, let's define a Delighter! A car that will allow you to dynamically change the exterior color on demand from your smartphone using a palette of five preset colors. This hypothetical example can be achieved by using programable ink coatings technology when the car was manufactured. The car owner could choose the desired color with their smartphone by plugging into a special port on the dashboard. Providing this feature to a specific car market will delight and excite some customers, and they are willing to pay the extra premium to receive this added value attribute. If these same customers were not offered this value-added attribute, they would be neutral about its absence. The next example is a real product. White ceiling paint is difficult to apply and know if it was properly covering the older white paint since it is typically white on white. A new ceiling paint was developed. When the paint is applied, it goes on purple to know exactly the areas that have been painted. Once the painted purple-colored ceiling dried, it changed to white. Customers that used this type of paint were extremely happy since it addressed a hidden or latent need that the customer experienced, and the paint manufacturer offered an unexpected solution.

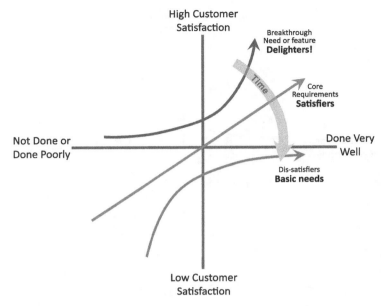

FIGURE 2.10
Kano model with all three categories: Basic Needs, Satisfiers, and Delighters!

It is important to note that these arrows get demoted with time. What used to be a Delighter! at one time becomes a Satisfier, and subsequently a Satisfier becomes a Basic Need (Figure 2.10). Many years ago, hotel rooms did not offer a refrigerator. When they were first available, it was a Delighter! The same can be said when an iron and ironing board was offered in hotel rooms. Today, these amenities are Satisfiers, and some may argue, they are now Basic Needs. An example of a Satisfier for an automobile is the car door locks. They started as keyed door locks and advanced to push-button wireless locks. The first generation of push-button wireless door entries was directional using an infrared beam; you needed to point to the inside dome light of the vehicle through the glass window to open or lock the doors. The next-generation keyless entries developed were omnidirectional using a radio frequency to unlock the doors. As you approach the vehicle, you can unlock its doors many feet away. Today, the latest system unlocks the car based on proximity to the driver seat. By just having the key fob entry in our pocket, the car automatically unlocks, and the door opens freely. Today the key fob is a Delighter! The previous generation push-button wireless key entry has migrated from being a Satisfier to a Basic Need, and now the original key entry is antiquated and used

TABLE 2.2

Comparing the Three Kano Model Categories

Basic Needs	Satisfiers	Delighters!
Expected attributes or needs	Attributes that make you competitive in the market	Unexpected attributes or needs
Attribute not met: customer will be extremely dissatisfied	Attribute not met: customer will be dissatisfied	Attribute not met: customer is neutral about it, doesn't know about it
Attribute met: the most the customer would feel is neutral about that attribute or need	Attribute met: the customer is more satisfied about it, more is better	Attribute met: customer satisfaction level will soar
Often unspoken needs, assumed to be there	Typically, these are spoken, used in advertisements, packaging, etc.	Mostly unspoken needs
Best collected: one-on-one interviews, focus groups	Best collected: using surveys	Best collected: one-on-one interviews, focus groups

for emergencies only. Many years ago, the air conditioner in a car was considered a luxury Delighter! today it is a must have, Basic Need.

In conclusion, we learned that customers can be very demanding and product manufacturers need to stay attuned to their client's needs either spoken or unspoken. Table 2.2 summarizes the three Kano model categories highlighting their similarities and differences.

2.4 USING THE KANO MODEL: EXPLANATION OF SUCCESS

We have outlined the Kano model, and its three key categories are defined as: Basic Needs, Satisfiers, and Delighters! We will now use the data from our fictitious company, Liquid Paint Specialists, to convert the top attributes into specific questions that will be constructed and used during the one-on-one interviews with Tubing Experts. Figure 2.11 shows the process flow for the conversion of top attributes to Kano questions. These interviews will combine two answers of the customer's feelings of the product with different performance attributes.

Converting the one-word or two-word attributes to questions for the interviews will need to be carefully constructed. It would be best to have

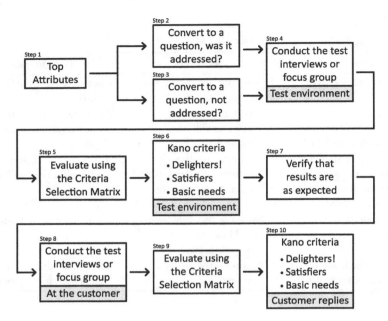

FIGURE 2.11
Process flow, converting top attributes to Kano questions.

the core team that defined the attributes of the product to compose these requests. Each attribute will create two questions. One will emphasize addressing the situation, and the other is contrarian, it doesn't address the condition. For example, using our fourth-ranked attribute, *samples*, from our Pareto chart from Liquid Paint Specialists as seen in Figure 2.4, we can now construct the two questions based on the formulaic structure shown in Figure 2.12a.

Sometimes the single word needs to be expanded to provide the right context. From the brainstorming session, we had the word *samples.*

(a) How would you feel if _____ _____?
            (Attribute)   (was addressed)

How would you feel if _____ _____?
            (Attribute)   (was not addressed)

(b) How would you feel if *your supplier has a useful product sampling process*?
            (Attribute)   (was addressed)

How would you feel if *your supplier has an inferior product sampling process*?
            (Attribute)   (was not addressed)

FIGURE 2.12
(a) Converting attributes into the two interview questions. (b) Example converting attributes into the two interview questions.

In this case, *samples* refer to product samples offered to the customer for tests or trials; it could have meant the reverse, samples given from our customer to us. That is the main reason why the team must collaboratively agree on the wording structure of the enquiries. As shown in the accompanying Figure 2.12b, the attribute placeholder can be substituted for a statement and not just a single word. We now convert the single word *sample* with the help of our team yielding the following: "if your supplier has a useful/inferior product sample process."

Putting the attribute in the format suggested in Figure 2.12b yields the following two questions: How would you feel if your supplier has a useful product sample process? How would you feel if your supplier has an inferior product sample process? As mentioned earlier, these questions combine the two dimensions of feeling and product performance. Since the queries bracket the results by addressing and not addressing the attribute's performance, we can now learn from the customer's perspective how they will respond. This is important since their response will translate to one of the three types of Kano categories: Basic Needs, Satisfiers, and Delighters! In rare occasions, these results may not translate into one of those three types which we will explore shortly.

Reverting to the Liquid Paint Specialists case study, the top four attributes from the Pareto chart in Figure 2.4 will be converted into the two interviewing questions. Starting with the highest rated product development, the team decided that we may want to learn various aspects of it, leading to three new sub-attributes. The first sub-attribute is to create a new product joint venture with our R&D and their team. We currently do not offer this service. Converting this sub-attribute into the two questions following the pattern of Figure 2.12a becomes: How would you feel if we jointly develop a new product? How would you feel if we don't jointly develop a new product? These questions will be used later as part of the focus group or interview with the customer. Creating sub-attributes helps us define and hone into deeper supplier/customer relationships, addressing potential new needs. Table 2.3 shows attributes and sub-attributes that we will explain throughout this section.

We continue with our team on how to articulate the two other sub-attributes of product development, starting with "develop a leading-edge product for you." Our team composed the two opposing questions from this new sub-attribute. How would you feel if we develop a leading-edge product for you? How would you feel if we don't develop a leading-edge product? The third and last sub-attribute of product development

TABLE 2.3

Attributes and Sub-attributes

Votes	Attributes	Sub-attributes
6	Product development	Jointly develop a new product
		Develop a leading-edge product for you
		Our product would increase your current rating on consumer reviews
5	Product consistency	Product is within specs
		Our product improves your productivity

is: a new product that will improve your current ratings on consumer reviews. Crafting those interview questions using the Kano structure yielded the following two questions. How would you feel if our product would increase your current rating on consumer reviews? How would you feel if our product would reduce your current rating on consumer reviews?

Let us now return to our Pareto chart in Figure 2.4. The second highest rated attribute from the Pareto chart, product consistency, created a similar discussion as the first rated attribute and derived two enhanced needs: product specifications and productivity. Refer to Table 2.3 to see these sub-attributes. Product specification was straightforward and yielded the following inquires: How do you feel if our product is within specs? How do you feel if our product is not in spec? Productivity, on the other hand, was taking a more creative approach to craft the questions. This productivity was with respect to improvements of our customer's productivity and not ours. Converting this sub-attribute using our format provided these two Kano questions: How do you feel if our product improves your productivity? How do you feel if our product does not increase your productivity?

The third main attribute, delivery, generated the following: How would you feel if your shipment arrived when you want it? How would you feel if your shipment arrived other than the time when you want it? This second question could have been reworded, how would you feel if your shipment arrived earlier than the time you want it? Some companies may find receiving the product ahead of schedule to be acceptable. On the other hand, for some companies that run their facilities just-in-time, the second question may not be satisfactory. They may have a very tight supply chain, with specific arrival times and loading docks availability. If we do not deliver within the allotted time plus-minus a small window of opportunity, we may lose our slot and our customer will not receive the product as expected. As this example shows, make sure that you look at all angles on how to word these questions, capturing our capabilities plus our customer's desired needs.

2.5 CONVERT THE REPLIES TO KANO CRITERIA

At this point, all interviewing questions are prepared and ready to test the responses. We follow the process shown in Figure 2.11, and test Step 6 of the flowchart. Selecting people from our company, we stress tested our questions, creating an environment that will allow honest and candid feedback. We learned that all interviewing questions were properly interpreted as they were intended. We will allow only four types of responses: good, typical, neutral, and not good. Let's explore the following replies as we refer to Figure 2.13.

To understand how this chart can be used with the responses from our interview, we need to recall that these are paired questions, one is addressing the situation and the second is not, in other words, not addressing the situation. Let's detail how this chart is used by demonstrating it with an example. Our company team members, testing our questions with a mock interview, provided the following answers. The first question addressing the situation was answered *neutral*, and the second question not addressing the situation was replied *not good*. That specific combination yields a Basic Need as shown in Figure 2.13. You'll find that depending on how the combination of those replies will deliver one of the three Kano categories using the criteria selection matrix.

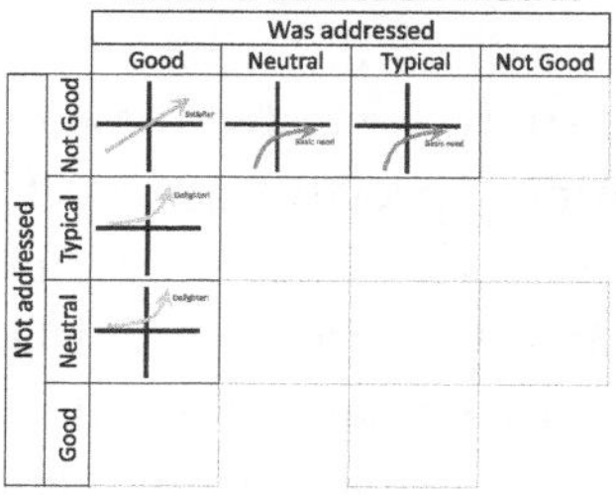

FIGURE 2.13
Criteria selection matrix, converting the two questions' replies into Kano categories.

Notice that in Figure 2.13 only 5 from all 16 possible combinations are significant. Looking at those five, two become Delighters! two others are Basic Needs, and only one is a Satisfier. When these questions are used in interviews with customers, the most common answers are Satisfiers followed by Basic Needs and the least common ones are Delighters! That distribution of categories will vary from industry to industry and product to product. In addition, you are not at the mercy of statistical probabilities to have your interviews be answered in that manner. Since you are crafting these questions with a carefully selected multifunctional team, you and your team can create answers that may spark more Delighters! and less Basic Needs.

As mentioned earlier, we may have situations that will create a combination of results that do not map to any of those three Kano categories. Let us explore these potential cases with an example. After going through an internal brainstorming session with your company employees, you and your team discovered that our customer will benefit by having a straight-line communication to our Quality Control (QC) department. This attribute was then converted into the following two Kano questions. How would you feel if the name, phone, and email information of our QC representative were included in our Certificate of Analysis, COA? How would you feel if the name, phone, and email information of our QC representative were not included in our COA? When these queries were asked during the customer focus group sessions, the team received the following responses. The first answer, related to addressing the attribute of having the QC information, gave a result of neutral. The second reply from our client, if the attribute was not addressed, was typical. Using the diagram shown in Figure 2.13, the intersection of these two answers takes us in an unmapped area. This attribute is not a customer need. It is not value added, and we should not put resources on it. This is an important finding and must be discussed carefully with your team when debriefing all these close-ended questions.

Returning to our case study, we tested these questions with our internal team at Liquid Coatings Specialist using a focused group approach. After reviewing the answers, the Kano categories that emerged from the one-on-one assessment interviews yielded satisfactory results. Our team felt confident to use this questionnaire with our customer Tubing Experts. Table 2.4 shows all the close-ended Kano questions that will be used during the customer visit.

TABLE 2.4

Completed Kano Questions

Votes	Attributes	Was Addressed	Not Addressed
6	Product development	How would you feel if we jointly develop a new product?	How would you feel if we don't jointly develop a new product?
		How would you feel if we develop a leading-edge product for you?	How would you feel if we don't develop a leading-edge product?
		How would you feel if our product would increase your current rating on consumer reviews?	How would you feel if our product would reduce your current rating on consumer reviews?
5	Product consistency	How do you feel if our product is within specs?	How do you feel if our product is not in spec?
		How do you feel if our product improves your productivity?	How do you feel if our product does not increase your productivity?
4	Delivery (on time)	How would you feel if your shipment arrived when you want it?	How would you feel if your shipment arrived other than the time when you want it?
4	Samples	How would you feel if your supplier has a useful product sample process?	How would you feel if your supplier has an inferior product sample process?

This chapter defined close-ended questions that will be used to gather the voice of the customer. In addition, we tested these two bracketed enquiries that led to two answers. After decoding those responses, they defined the Kano categories of Basic Needs, Satisfiers, or Delighters! Later in Chapter 5, we will use these top attributes to create the first House of Quality.

3

Gather Metrics for Success (Our Customer's Perspective)

In this chapter, we will define and gather the Voice of the Customer (VOC), starting with open-ended questions. The scope needs to be narrow since open-ended inputs may diverge and take us away from our intended purpose. These questions will provide more definition about our product and how our company is perceived. Later, we will complement the information with the close-ended Kano questions.

3.1 PREPARE FOR THE CUSTOMER INTERVIEW

Prior to the customer interview, our fictitious companies have had several conversations. These talks were done ahead of time before we participated on the data gathering of the VOC. These conversations are normally made by our commercial team mainly from the sales or marketing department. The intent is to create an atmosphere of collaboration and a two-way communication between the customer and our team. Qualitative research of our client is best done in person, face-to-face, in their offices, or in their facilities. Anticipate about 1–2 hours to conduct the interviews. During that visit, a plant or facility tour could be arranged to further understand how the product is being used during the manufacturing process. After all, it is our product in the factory they are using.

In preparation for the customer interview, we need to determine ahead of time how many of our employees will be going to the visit. Some of the key contributors would include a designated facilitator (selected by the core team), a person from manufacturing, sales, and marketing.

You may consider the original eight that participated in the brainstorming and Kano exercise. In addition, you may want to add two or three employees, but take care not to make such a large group that it might be intimidating to the customer, especially if they have a smaller group.

Next, define which method to gather the VOC. You can gather customer information using one-on-one interviews or focus groups. Which option is chosen will mainly be a personal choice suggested either by our team or by the customer. An alternative option would be to use both methods. The one-on-one interviews use the Kano questions and the focus group uses the open-ended queries. A third possibility would be to do both open- and close-ended questionnaires in a focus group to encourage dialog and freely exchange ideas in an orderly manner.

The location of the interview should be at the customer's site. It can be at their factory, but it needs to be in an area that is removed from day-to-day activities. The best results occur when the customer is completely immersed and not distracted during these sessions. The number of client team members involved should be as many as they are willing to afford. Similar to the rule of thumb we used earlier, a manageable team is between 7 and 12 people. If the customer provides more people, then that clearly speaks to the level of their commitment and your team did an outstanding job convincing them of the importance of such a visit.

3.1.1 How Do You Define Success?

Success is defined from the customer's perspective regarding our product. The prework needed to define the open-ended questions shouldn't be as arduous as the close-ended ones. We only need to define key topics and let the customer fill in the details. In the previous chapter, those questionnaires took longer since it was our perception of the customer. We needed to probe with many questions to focus on our topic.

A key question to ask the customer is, what did they find important about using our product? Depending on who you ask different viewpoints will be given. Capturing verbatim what the customer values is imperative. They may reply with a combination of *needs* and *wants*. Let's be clear, *needs* are attributes or conditions that must be met. These conditions help make a basic quality product or to comply with government or industry regulations. *Wants*, on the other hand, are less authoritative; these are metrics or conditions that are nice to have. As we have done before when we introduce a concept, an illustration would help bring a different

TABLE 3.1

List of Needs and Wants

Needs	Wants
All your nonconformance issues should use SCAR, Supplier Corrective Action Request	The coating can be applied at the temperature range of −15°F to 105°F
Color match is ≤0.8 delta E_{cmc}	The heavier product should be packed first on the truck to reduce damage
Particle size 2 ± 0.1 mils	Particle size 2 ± 0.001 mils
1 or 2 peels or cracks per 100 linear ft	Your coating should account for 10% of our unscheduled downtime
Gloss is 85% at 60°	I would like to have a product that has low odor

perspective to the topic. Table 3.1 provides examples of a few needs and wants.

Returning to our case study example of Tubing Experts, let's learn what type of questions we will prepare to ask our client. As we gather the core team of eight participants, we brainstormed a few ideas and jotted down on a whiteboard a few open-ended topics.

As seen in Figure 3.1, the list is not too long. We want to keep the topics short and focused. We will present each question to the customer one at a time, and then they will provide multiple answers for each one. After this dialog is completed, using the focus group, we will then wrap up the conversation with one last request. If you could select the ultimate metric of success, which of these replies will you choose?

Depending on the dynamics of the customer team, you may encounter a situation which a single metric becomes so dominant that everyone agrees on it. Consider that a blessing since now you have the key metric that the customer uses to define success. If this ideal situation does not present itself at your customer's meeting, you may want to perform a multi-vote

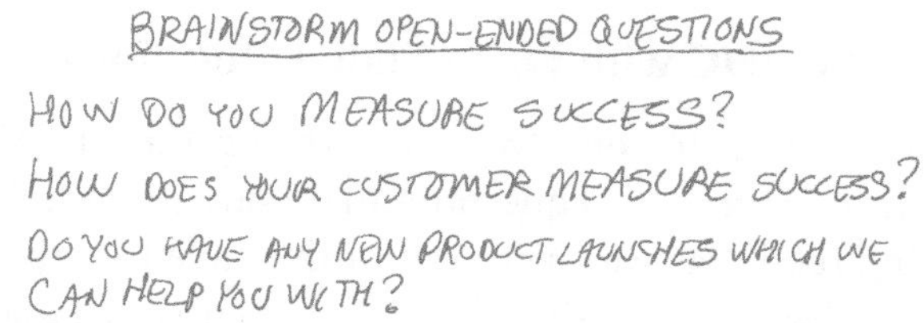

FIGURE 3.1
Brainstorming a few open-ended topics to ask our customer.

as discussed in Chapter 2 for selecting top attributes. As a suggestion, the selected facilitator should guide the customer team to choose the topic with the most votes.

3.2 CONDUCT THE INTERVIEW

We now have the entire framework to gather the open- and close-ended questions from our customer. At this point, all preparations for the appropriate location have been selected. The format for the question-naires will be done with both one-on-one interviews and focus group style. For many weeks, our team has been preparing for this moment. It's showtime!

Finally, the day has arrived and our team from Liquid Paint Specialists arrives at the Tubing Experts headquarters. They are located near their largest manufacturing plant which makes the most use of the product we supply. Sitting in the conference room, we noticed that their team comprises of eight people; that is an equal match to the number of people we brought from our company. This total of 16 is slightly more than the suggested 12 participants, making the coordination a little bit more challenging.

After the preliminary handshakes and introductions, we begin to share our agenda on how we plan to conduct the VOC data gathering. As previously scheduled, we visit the manufacturing plant. The plant tour satisfies two objectives. First, it gives us a direct view on how the product is being applied at the facility which helps us understand any nuances of its uses and applications. Second, and more importantly, it is a great icebreaker. Getting to know your customer in person establishes a bond that transcends any type of phone call or video conferencing.

3.2.1 Gather the VOC with Open-Ended Questions

After the conclusion of the tour, we will start to gather the VOC, beginning with the three open-ended questions in a focus group style. They gave us the following replies as we went around the table listening to each of the contributors. Tables 3.2–3.4 show the list of open-ended questions with customer's responses.

TABLE 3.2

First Open-Ended Question with Customer's Responses

How Do You Measure Success?
No recordable safety incidents
Number of tubes we made today, our mileage for the day
The appearance of the coated surface looks good
Product is coated evenly at the desired thickness

TABLE 3.3

Second Open-Ended Question with Customer's Responses

How Does Your Customer Measure Success?
Our orders arrive on time and in full
They partner with us to make new products
Satisfaction and praises from the level of quality we provide to them

TABLE 3.4

Third Open-Ended Question with Customer's Responses

Do You Have Any New Product Launches Which We Can Help You with?
Yes, we have a new multiuse display. Our end user would like to use our product as a hands-on training for display structures

After all the answers were collected, which took about 20 minutes, the customer felt comfortable with the inquiries and how the dialog pace was going. Into the final stretch of questions, we asked for one last request: which response will you rate as the ultimate metric of success? As the customer team huddles to discuss among themselves which one will be the most impactful, our team overhears the word safety and customer satisfaction being tossed about. Finally, after a few moments, the Tubing Expert team emerges with the answer of mileage. We asked, why did mileage make it to the top of the list? The reply was that the people at the factory floor are given a bonus based on how many miles of quality tubes were produced on a given day under safe conditions. It was the singling out of mileage that surprised us. We would have never thought that mileage was such an impactful metric of success. Such is the importance of having a customer visit.

We have the ultimate metric. We now ask our customer for a couple more that have a medium impact. The Tubing Experts team provided us with their top three choices:

- Our orders arrive on time and in full.
- Appearance.
- Even coating thickness.

This concludes the gathering of the open-ended inquiries from our client. Next, we will gather the close-ended questions to complete the VOC.

3.2.2 Gather the VOC with Close-Ended Kano Questions

We finished collecting the open-ended replies and learned that the key metric for success is mileage. We will now conduct the interviews with the close-ended Kano questions. Recall that we, Liquid Paint Specialist, used the highest voted attributes, and we converted these into questions to know if that product attribute or feature "was addressed" or "was not addressed." The results from our customer interview are presented on Table 3.5. Depending on how the customer's paired responses are, we can convert these into one of the three Kano categories: Basic Needs, Satisfiers, and Delighters! Please refer to Figure 2.13 in Chapter 2 to see how these Kano categories are determined using the criteria selection matrix.

We have reached the end of the interviewing process and the gathering of the VOC. After all the pleasantries were exchanged with Tubing Experts, we left their offices after several hours. While our team was driving back to the airport, we debriefed what we had learned. The number one topic that kept shaking our head was the powerful and simple metric of success. Mileage.

3.3 COMBINE AND QUANTIFY THE VOCs

The raw data has been collected and it needs to be converted into meaningful information that will help us make decisions. This process involves distilling the open- and close-ended replies to the finer few which will become the first building blocks of House of Quality 1 (HOQ1).

TABLE 3.5

Close-Ended Kano Questions with Responses

Attributes	Was Addressed	Answer	Not Addressed	Answer	Kano Category
Product development	How would you feel if we jointly develop a new product?	Good	How would you feel if we don't jointly develop a new product?	Typical	Delighter!
	How would you feel if we develop a leading-edge product for you?	Good	How would you feel if we don't develop a leading-edge product?	Not good	Satisfier
	How would you feel if our product would increase your current rating on consumer reviews?	Good	How would you feel if our product would reduce your current rating on consumer reviews?	Not good	Satisfier
Product consistency	How do you feel if our product is within specs?	Neutral	How do you feel if our product is not in spec?	Not good	Basic Need
	How do you feel if our product increase your productivity?	Good	How do you feel if our product does not increase your productivity?	Typical	Delighter!
Delivery (on time)	How would you feel if your shipment arrived when you want it?	Neutral	How would you feel if your shipment arrived other than the time when you want it?	Not good	Basic Need
Samples	How would you feel if your supplier has a good product sample process?	Neutral	How would you feel if your supplier has a bad product sample process?	Not good	Basic Need

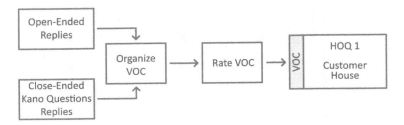

FIGURE 3.2
Organize the VOC from open- and closed-end questions.

Figure 3.2 shows a partial view of the process map that will help shape HOQ1. The last step shown in the diagram, using the VOCs in HOQ1, will be described in more detail in Chapter 5. In this section, we will finish with a list of prioritized VOCs.

We begin by using the most important open-ended response, mileage, and will give it a high rating of 9, using a three-leveled skewed rating scale of 9, 3, and 1. This rating will be used again when we complete HOQ1. Tubing Experts indicated during the open-ended replies that these three "our orders arrive on time and in full," "appearance," and "even coating thickness," were given a medium rating. We will move these three forward with a rating of 3.

Switching to the close-ended Kano questions, we will give a rating priority from highest to lowest depending on the Kano criteria. This 9-, 3-, 1- tilted scale makes Delighters! more important with a value of 9, thus making Satisfiers equal to 3 and Basic Needs 1. These results are summarized in Table 3.6. In addition, we added a column on the far right on the table to know if each line item has a direct relationship to product performance. This will help us know how to sort out these valuable nuggets of information given to us by our customer.

After reviewing the results from the Tubing Experts interviews and focus group discussions, the VOC that are not directly related to the product performance can be used to enhance the relationship between our company and our customer. Not all of these are going to be used on HOQ1, only those properties that are directly related to product performance. We will extract those that will be carried forward to HOQ1 as shown in Table 3.7.

We learned many facets from our customer through the structured and unstructured formats of our questions and interviews. This process provided us a glimpse from their perspective to know how to improve

TABLE 3.6

Open- and Close-Ended Kano Questions Ratings Summary

Main Attributes	Attributes/ Sub-attributes	Kano Category	Rating	Related to Product Performance
–	No recordable safety incidents	–	–	No
–	Mileage made today	–	9	Yes
–	Our orders arrive on time and in full	–	3	No
–	Appearance	–	3	Yes
–	Even coating thickness	–	3	Yes
Product development	Jointly develop a new product	Delighter!	9	No
	Develop a leading-edge product for you	Satisfier	3	No
	Our product would increase your current rating on consumer reviews	Satisfier	3	No
Product consistency	Product is within specs	Basic Need	1	Yes
	Our product improves your productivity	Delighter!	9	Yes
Delivery (on time)	Shipment arrived when you want it	Basic Need	1	No
Samples	Good product sample process	Basic Need	1	No

TABLE 3.7

VOCs that Will Be Carried Forward to HOQ1

Attributes/Sub-attributes	Kano Category	Rating	Related to Product Performance
Mileage made today	–	9	Yes
Appearance	–	3	Yes
Even coating thickness	–	3	Yes
Product is within specs	Basic Need	1	Yes
Our product improves your productivity	Delighter!	9	Yes

our product and product offerings that go beyond product performance. We are now positioned to move forward top five VOCs items. In Chapter 5, these VOCs will be used as the first building blocks to construct HOQ1.

4

Critical to Quality Metrics

In this chapter, we will be exploring quality metrics of the product. These metrics are either defined from the industry we serve or are inherent from the way the product performs. Later in this chapter, these product properties will be prepared for use in House of Quality 1 (HOQ1). In Chapter 5, these Critical to Quality (CTQ) metrics will be ranked based on the order of importance, using product performance as the standard for ranking.

4.1 DEFINE QUALITY METRICS

4.1.1 Industry Metrics

Quality metrics can be imposed by the specific industry we serve or performance testing done on the products being made. For example, if you are a producer of electrical metallic tubing or EMT steel conduit, these tubes are used in building infrastructure encasing electrical wires. Therefore, your product will need to follow the standards and guidelines of NEMA, the National Electrical Manufacturers Association. If you are in another industry, such as kitchen cabinets, the KCMA (Kitchen Cabinet Manufacturers Association) can provide product certifications based on quality tests and eco-friendly products. These certifications will differentiate your product since they have been tested according to the rigorous standards defined by KCMA. Additional steps may be obligatory for your industry or may be an optional choice to enhance your product offering. Whichever the case may be, it can provide the end user a level of competitiveness that may be worthwhile for your company to take the extra effort.

Sometimes these quality standards and certifications may not be enough to distinguish your product from others, you may choose to participate on having performance evaluation and ranking done by an organization that provides unbiased testing, certifications, or rankings. Of course, these types of tests need to be carefully selected and determined if it is viable for the type of product you offer. Some of these organizations may invite your company to participate, and you may choose to commit to these extra rigorous tests against your competitors. In addition, these qualifying bodies may offer certifications for that industry. Two prominent organizations that provide these types of services are Consumer Reports and UL (known formally as Underwriters Laboratories). Let's say, you are a producer of paint and you comfortably meet the industry standards and would like to have an extra advantage to have your product ranked with your competitors. Consumer Reports does precisely that, and they will rank from best overall performance paint to the least. They will even split it between interior paint and exterior paint. This ranking is done using many performance statistics and price, those values that have the best balancing of all these metrics make it to the top of the ranking. Needless to say, this type of unbiased accolade on your product will play very well for the discriminating end user.

Let us return to our case study, we are the supplier of paint coatings, and our customer is the one applying the brightly colored paint on plastic tubes. Since we are using a fictitious product and customer, we will also use fictitious industry standards. Our company, Liquid Paint Specialists, is part of the Liquid Paint Coating Industry, LPCI, and needs to follow the industry norms and standards of crack rates and cure time dictated by LPCI. Our customer, Tubing Experts, needs to follow the Plastic Tubing Association's (PTA) standards. PTA requires three different industry metrics: crack rates, cure time, and tubing flexibility. These metrics must be front and center when making these products since they are imposed by the industry that the product is made for. They are the first three parameters that define the CTQ metrics.

To know more about these CTQs, each one of these three metrics has a procedure that defines the acceptable levels of performance provided by LPCI. Starting with crack rates, we learn that it follows standard LPCI-123, which specifies the Standard Operating Procedure (SOP) on how the crack rate test is performed and evaluated. The acceptable crack rate test is 1 crack every 1,000 ft of production. The crack rate is determined by bending the painted tube 180° and evaluate if the paint cracked. This test becomes a specification we need to adhere to.

Moving along with the second CTQ, cure time, it follows standard LPCI-456. Similar to the previous standard, it contains the SOP and desired performance characteristics. In this case, the amount of time stipulated for the paint to cure is 120 seconds or less.

The third CTQ, tubing flexibility, uses standard PTA-007, and it has an SOP with its specification. This spec is a little more complex and it reads, "…a batch of tubes bent 180 degrees should have 90% of tube integrity…" This standard needs more interpretation. *A batch of tubes* is referring to a sampling technique. In the case of Tubing Experts, they gather ten tubes periodically from production to evaluate if at least nine tubes pass the 90% threshold. *Tube integrity* refers to several potential failures. The unpainted tube must maintain its cross-sectional round shape and not collapse during the bend. In addition, it must maintain a smooth clean bend with no cracks, splits, or tents. A summary of these results is shown in Table 4.1.

4.1.2 Customer Metrics: You Don't Know What You Don't Know

Measurements create commitments. When you measure, you start to know, and that knowledge can provide valuable information for a decision. Let's take that thinking to a different level. You step on a scale to reveal your weight. Now you know! That piece of information can take you two paths, either you gained weight or lost weight. If you gained weight, you had "too much fun" during the Thanksgiving holidays, you are surprised by the unexpected weight gain. The second reflects the new exercise and diet routines started 2 weeks ago; it is taking effect and you are happy. As shown in these two outcomes, the measurement helped confirm the assumptions of that elusive number, revealing and helping us know more about the decision we took or shouldn't have taken.

Let's expand on that cause-and-effect relationship between measurement and decisions with more examples. I look at my watch to know the

TABLE 4.1

CTQs from Industry Standards

Critical to Quality	Metric	Standard
Crack rates	1 crack per 1,000 ft	LPCI-123
Cure time	120 seconds or less	LPCI-456
Tube integrity	90% or better	PTA-007

time (measure). Will I make it on time to the meeting on the fifth floor? (decision) What's the temperature outside (measure), and will I need a coat and gloves (decision)? As seen in these events, measurements and decisions are everywhere. Most companies will measure their manufactured article along the way as it is being produced. The sampling and measurement techniques may occur from the very early stages of product creation all the way to the final test. Learning about the key steps and metrics that the customer tracks when using our supplied raw materials reveals what is important to them; it becomes a key metric.

Tubing Experts very closely track five metrics in their manufacturing line that relates to our supplied paint for their tube manufacturing. These five are: *plugged spray nozzles, consistency of cured film build, sticky tubes, plugged filters,* and *holiday testing.* Each variable is monitored and tracked by our technical sales support team during the routine visits at the customer's plant. Keeping a close eye on these five key numbers gives us a good glimpse of their production process, ensuring high-quality painted tubes emerge from the finishing line of their factory.

Let's learn how each of these customer variables is defined. Figure 4.1 shows the process steps and where along that process the measurement is taken as the tube is being manufactured.

Starting with the spray booth, we find two variables being measured in this area: *plugged spray nozzles* and *plugged filters.* The tubes are made in the extruder and are being formed in a continuous manner without interruption, like a garden hose albeit more rigid. Immediately after the tube is coated, it passes through the paint booth, and the paint spray nozzle coats the tube in a nonstop manner which enters to the next unit operation, the oven, where the freshly coated tube will get cured. Since this tube is moving constantly, the nozzles need to provide a uniform spray pattern; in addition, the paint filters collect any debris that may cause a change in

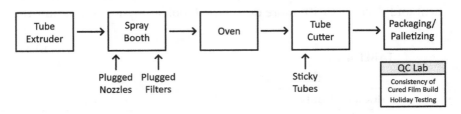

FIGURE 4.1
Customer's process block flow diagram.

the pattern or potentially restrict the flow of paint. The evaluation of the clogging of the spray nozzles is done visually and given a three-level rating of cleanliness using the stop-light visual cues: red = partly clogged, yellow = minimum clogging, and green = clean nozzle. These stop-light work instructions are on the factory floor with sample pictures of the nozzles to show the three levels of defects. In a comparable manner, the paint filters have a dial that indicate when these filters need to be changed. These units have a pressure dial across the filter, and on the dial, there is a red arrow at the value of 2 psi, as shown in Figure 4.2. When the filter reaches this value, it is time to change the filter. This pressure dial is monitored routinely as part of the paint nozzle checks.

Moving along the block diagram, the tube cutter will cut the tubes to the desired length. Typically, the tube is cut to the length of 10 ft. To perform this cut, the tube is being held by an automated jaw that will travel along at the speed of the tube while the saw cuts it and drops after a fraction of a second. After that very quick cut, the 10-ft tube rolls to the next unit operation for packaging and palletizing. *Sticky tubes* occur when the painted tube didn't dry or cure well enough. While the jaw holds it during the cutting process, several issues may contribute in not having the paint to be fully cured by the time it reaches the cutter. This is one of the main reasons we look at a key variable that consolidates many dependent conditions which could affect *sticky tubes*. This value is binary, either it is sticky showing signs of the tube adhering to the jaws of the cutting mechanism

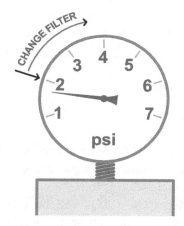

FIGURE 4.2
Pressure dial to change filters.

or it is not sticking, and the tube is released freely, rolling down to the packaging and palletizing area. If there is an issue with sticky tubes, then an investigation of the many potential causes needs to be conducted.

The last two metrics from our customer process measured in the Quality Control lab are *consistency of cured film build* and *holiday testing*. The first one, *consistency of cured film build*, is measured under the microscope by looking at a cross-sectional cut of the tube and measured at 90° angles. These four values are measured in mils. The specification for each measurement is 1.0 mils (0.025 mm) with a tolerance of ±0.3 mils. The second QC lab metric is the *holiday testing*. Holidays are defined as pinholes and voids on a painted thin-film coating. Typically, these pinholes can range from 1 to 10 mils (0.025–0.254 mm) in diameter. These holidays are counted and recorded under a microscope over a fixed surface area, expressing the results as a percent of pinholes or voids present. The acceptable range is between 0% and 1% maximum. Table 4.2 summarizes all the metrics from the customer's process.

TABLE 4.2

CTQs from Tubing Experts' Process

Critical to Quality	Metric	Process Area
Plugged spray nozzles	Red = partly clogged Yellow = minimum clogging Green = clean nozzle	Spray booth
Plugged filters	0–2 psi (>2 change)	Spray booth
Sticky tubes	Yes or no	Tube cutter
Consistency of cured film build	1.0 ± 0.3 mil	Quality control lab
Holiday testing	0% and 1%	Quality control lab

4.2 ORGANIZE CTQs

All CTQ metrics have been gathered from the standards imposed by the industry and from the customer manufacturing process. A summary of all CTQs is shown in Table 4.3.

As mentioned earlier, these CTQs will be used in building HOQ1. Figure 4.3 shows a flow diagram on how this will be used later in Chapter 5 to build HOQ1.

TABLE 4.3

All CTQs for Tubing Experts

Critical to Quality	Metric
Crack rates	1 crack per 1,000 ft
Cure time	120 seconds or less
Tube integrity	90% or better
Plugged spray nozzles	Red = partly clogged Yellow = minimum clogging Green = clean nozzle
Plugged filters	0–2 psi (>2 change)
Sticky tubes	Yes or no
Consistency of cured film build	1.0 ± 0.3 mil
Holiday testing	0% and 1%

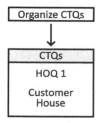

FIGURE 4.3
Organizing the CTQs for HOQ1.

5

Create House of Quality 1, the Customer House

We will accomplish a major milestone in this chapter, completing the House of Quality 1 (HOQ1). To reach this point, we did a tremendous amount of data gathering. The past few chapters guided us on how to collect information from our customer. We gathered the Voice of the Customer (VOC) data and the Critical to Quality (CTQ) metrics. These came from surveys and observations, some were objective, others subjective. The main point is that we were able to make the results quantifiable. At first, these looked like loosely related items. Now we will give it shape, combining these metrics by building HOQ1. Since all this data is coming from the customer, this first House of Quality is also referred to as the Customer House.

5.1 ORGANIZE THE VOC AND CTQs

Merging the VOCs and CTQs together will allow us to analyze and see our customer in a new dimension. The process flow diagram in Figure 5.1 shows how we plan to combine the VOCs and CTQs. These combined groups of variables resemble a matrix, building the first room of our House of Quality. It is important to know in which order these are placed. At the top are the CTQs and at the left are the VOCs. After they are arranged in this manner, we will rate the VOCs versus the CTQs, placing each combination of those results inside the grid of the first room.

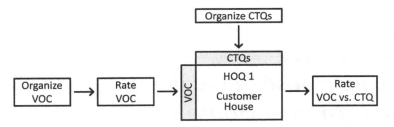

FIGURE 5.1
Process flow, making HOQ1.

5.2 COMBINE THE VOC AND THE CTQs

In Chapter 3, the Liquid Paint Specialists were hard at work collecting the top five VOCs from our customer, Tubing Experts. The data shown in Table 5.1 will be used as the first building block in the construction of HOQ1. We will be using the VOC's descriptions and associated ratings; these will be inserted into HOQ1 as shown in Figure 5.2.

After the VOCs have been placed in the house, we will now insert the CTQs on the top of the main room in HOQ1. Back in Chapter 4, we distilled from many sources eight key Customer Quality metrics. Table 5.2 highlights those eight key CTQs with their descriptions, the target value, desired ranges, and unit of measure that will be used to build the House of Quality. A new variable is being added from the original CTQs data: *directionality for improvement*. This added data can have three options: the first one is, the bigger the number, the better it is for the product. The second one is the opposite, the smaller the number, the better. The third one is a target or specific value within an allowable range. Let's see how this works with the CTQ of *Crack rates*. The lower the number of cracks counted, the better it is for the performance of the product. Other metrics may need to

TABLE 5.1
VOCs for HOQ1

Attributes/Sub-attributes	Rating
Product is within specs	1
Our product improves your productivity	9
Mileage made today	9
Even coating thickness	3
Appearance	3

House of Quality 1
Customer House

Metric improvement direction or target →									
Critical to Quality Metric, Target and Unit of Measure →									
Voice of Customer Wants/ Needs	Weight/ Priority								
Product is within specs.	1								
Our product improves your productivity.	9								
Mileage made today.	9								
Even coating thickness.	3								
Appearance.	3								

FIGURE 5.2
VOCs added to HOQ1.

hit a specific target value with a tolerance range; this definition is used on *Consistency of cured film build*. These extra characteristics for the CTQs have been added as a new column in Table 5.2 and will be placed in HOQ1 as shown in Figure 5.3.

5.2.1 Build the Main Room of HOQ1

HOQ1 is starting to take shape. We are now ready to combine the CTQs with the VOCs. The order on how to interpret this relationship is significant as shown with the direction of the arrow in Figure 5.4.

TABLE 5.2
CTQs for HOQ1

Critical to Quality	Metric	Metric Improvement Direction or Target
Crack rates	1 crack per 1,000 ft	Lower is better
Cure time	120 seconds or less	Target
Tube integrity	Minimum 90%	Higher is better
Plugged spray nozzles	Red = partly clogged Yellow = minimum clogging Green = clean nozzle	Higher is better
Plugged filters	0–2 psi (>2 change)	Lower is better
Sticky tubes	Yes or no	Target
Consistency of cured film build	1.0 ± 0.3 mil	Target
Holiday testing	0% and 1%	Lower is better

House of Quality 1
Customer House

Metric improvement direction or target →		▼	•	▲	▲	▼	•	•	▼	
Critical to Quality Metric, Target and Unit of Measure →		1 crack per 1000ft	120 seconds or less	Minimum 90%	Red = partly clogged, Yellow = min clogging, Green = clean	0 to 2 psi (>2 change)	Yes or No	1.0 mil +/- 0.3 mil	0% and 1%	
Voice of Customer Wants/ Needs	Weight / Priority	Crack rates	Cure time	Tube integrity	Plugged spray nozzles	Plugged filters	Sticky tubes	Consistency of cured film build	Holiday testing	
Product is within specs.	1									
Our product improves your productivity.	9									
Mileage made today.	9									
Even coating thickness.	3									
Appearance.	3									

FIGURE 5.3
CTQs and unit of measures added to HOQ1.

These arrows show the directional thought process by asking, how does vertical arrow affect the horizontal arrow? Let's translate this by using the actual CTQ and VOC. How does *Crack rates* affect *No Cracking*? This relationship seems obvious and highly correlated, so we will use the scale in Figure 5.4 and reply with a strong relationship (using the table it translates to the value of 9). This scale is an expanded version of 9, 3, and 1 scale we used earlier in Chapter 3 for the Kano ratings. This rating range has extra mid values between the 9 and the 3 and another mid value between 3 and 1, creating the 9, 6, 3, 2, and 1 scale. As before, the scale is skewed making the higher values to be more distinct and separated from the mid and lower values.

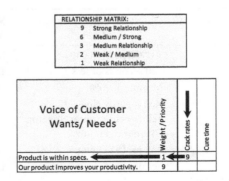

RELATIONSHIP MATRIX:
9	Strong Relationship
6	Medium / Strong
3	Medium Relationship
2	Weak / Medium
1	Weak Relationship

Voice of Customer Wants/ Needs	Weight / Priority	Crack rates	Cure time
Product is within specs. ⟵	1 ⟵	9	
Our product improves your productivity.	9		

FIGURE 5.4
How to rate the relationship of a CTQ with a VOC in HOQ1.

Voice of Customer Wants/ Needs	Weight / Priority	Crack rates	Cure time	Tube integrity	Plugged spray nozzles	Plugged filters	Sticky tubes	Consistency of cured film build	Holiday testing	
Product is within specs.	1	9		6		1		6	6	
Our product improves your productivity.	9		9	9	3		9	6	9	
Mileage made today.	9	3	9	9	9	1	9	9	9	
Even coating thickness.	3			9	9			9	9	
Appearance.	3			3	3	1		3	1	

FIGURE 5.5
Completed main room of HOQ1.

The best way to fill this House of Quality room is starting with the left-most column and going down the rows one by one to assess each VOC. Advance to the next column and repeat this cycle until all columns have been evaluated and rated with each VOC. As noted in Figure 5.5, the completed first room of the house doesn't have all boxes filled out with a number. You are not forced to place a value if no relationship exists between that CTQ and VOC.

5.2.2 Rank the VOCs

The VOCs are now ready to be interpreted in a different light, by using their importance and how they are influenced by different dependent factors. Those factors are the ones we just completed in showing the relationships between CTQ and VOC. Look at the filled-out table in Figure 5.5 and noticed which row has more numbers in it, and of those numbers, which VOC has more 9s and 6s than others. This cursory approach will be a good first start in identifying the most influential VOCs. Now that we have created a picture in our mind about those high and low VOC values, we will compute each VOC to know numerically which one is more important. The calculations are outlined in Figure 5.6. The most significant one has a VOC importance factor of 522, *Mileage made today.*

Reverting to the VOC interviews in Chapter 3, at that time, we were surprised that Tubing Experts were using *Mileage* as a key metric for their plant performance. By analyzing the VOCs and CTQs, we learned more about what the customer deemed more important, aligning us more with their needs and wants. In our calculation, we notice that after completing the main room on HOQ1, *Mileage made today* became the number 1 VOC followed by *our product improves your productivity.* Both VOCs being

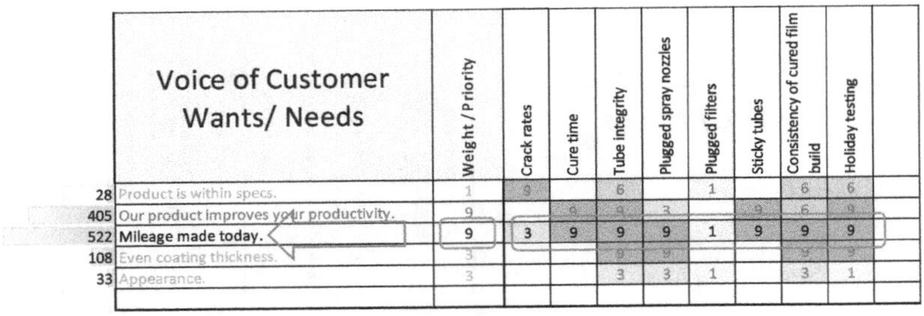

Voice of Customer Wants/ Needs	Weight / Priority	Crack rates	Cure time	Tube integrity	Plugged spray nozzles	Plugged filters	Sticky tubes	Consistency of cured film build	Holiday testing	
28 Product is within specs.	1	9			6		1	6	6	
405 Our product improves your productivity.	9		9	9	3		9	6	9	
522 Mileage made today.	9	3	9	9	9	1	9	9	9	
108 Even coating thickness.	3				9	9		9	9	
33 Appearance.	3			3	3	1		3	1	

CTQ Importance = Weight × Sum (CTQs)
CTQ Importance = 9×(3+9+9+9+1+9+9+9)
CTQ Importance = 9×58
CTQ Importance = 522

FIGURE 5.6
How the VOCs importance bar chart is calculated in HOQ1.

highly rated are now no surprise to us since it matches what we learned from our customer visit and data analysis. What makes this validation important is it confirms and expands our understanding of key metrics and how they impact our customer in a proactive manner.

5.2.3 Rank the CTQs

The VOCs are now completed and ranked from the highest to lowest. We will now rank the CTQ metrics in a comparable manner. The CTQs will follow the formula shown in Figure 5.7. As noted in the equation, it will use the different weights of the VOCs to determine how the CTQ is impacted.

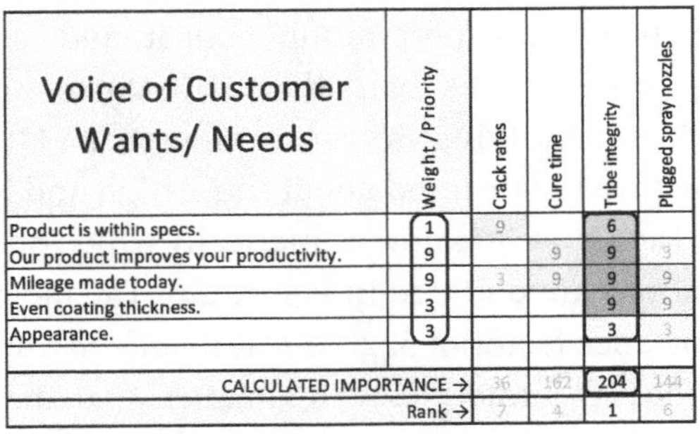

Voice of Customer Wants/ Needs	Weight / Priority	Crack rates	Cure time	Tube integrity	Plugged spray nozzles
Product is within specs.	1	9		6	
Our product improves your productivity.	9		9	9	3
Mileage made today.	9	3	9	9	9
Even coating thickness.	3			9	9
Appearance.	3			3	3
CALCULATED IMPORTANCE →		36	162	204	144
Rank →		7	4	1	6

CTQ Importance = SumProduct CTQs
CTQ Importance = Sum (Weights × CTQs)
CTQ Importance = (1×6)+(9×9)+(9×9)+(3×9)+(3×3)
CTQ Importance = 204

FIGURE 5.7
How the CTQs importance is calculated in HOQ1.

House of Quality 1
Customer House

Metric improvement direction or target →		Crack rates	Cure time	Tube integrity	Plugged spray nozzles	Plugged filters	Sticky tubes	Consistency of cured film build	Holiday testing
Critical to Quality Metric, Target and Unit of Measure →		▼ 1 crack per 1000ft	• 120 seconds or less	▲ Minimum 90%	▲ Red = partly clogged, Yellow = min clogging, Green = clean	▼ 0 to 2 psi (>2 change)	• Yes or No	• 1.0 mil +/- 0.3 mil	▼ 0% and 1%
Voice of Customer Wants/ Needs	Weight / Priority								
28 Product is within specs.	1	9		6		1		6	6
405 Our product improves your productivity.	9		9	9	3			6	9
522 Mileage made today.	9	3	9	9	9	1	9	9	9
108 Even coating thickness.	3			9	9			9	9
33 Appearance.	3			3	3	1		3	1
CALCULATED IMPORTANCE →		36	162	204	144	13	162	177	198
Rank →		7	4	1	6	8	5	3	2

FIGURE 5.8
Completed CTQs and VOCs in HOQ1.

The highest CTQ importance has a value of 204 belonging to *Tube integrity*. The bottom of HOQ1 has the ranking number for each of the CTQs ranging from number 1 for *Tube integrity* down to number 8 for *plugged filters* with a CTQ importance value of 13. The completed ranking is shown in Figure 5.8.

5.2.4 House of Quality 1

As we learned earlier, the impact of the VOCs confirms and quantifies our interview questions and customer visits. Similarly, the CTQs provide us a priority on how to focus on what the customer deems important. Perhaps a better way to visualize the CTQ rankings would be to have a Pareto chart with the percent impact of each CTQ as shown in Figure 5.9. The top CTQ has a value of 18.6%. The next five are similar in magnitude between 13% and 18%; however, the last two show a significant drop. One interesting point about the second to last CTQ, *Crack rates,* is near the bottom. This is an interesting finding: the customer doesn't have to explicitly tell us that they want tubes that don't crack. It is like the coffee shop story in Chapter 1, where the clients were enjoying their stay for several other reasons that weren't initially obvious. Nobody in the shop said they wanted hot coffee

CTQ Rank	Critical to Quality Metrics	Relative Weight (% impact)
1	Tube integrity	18.6%
2	Holiday testing	18.1%
3	Consistency of cured film build	16.1%
4	Cure time	14.8%
5	Sticky tubes	14.8%
6	Plugged spray nozzles	13.1%
7	Crack rates	3.3%
8	Plugged filters	1.2%

FIGURE 5.9
CTQ rankings Pareto chart.

in clean cups. Using our Kano definitions, hot coffee and clean cups are Basic Needs and so is *Crack rates* for Tubing Experts.

This information helps proactively understand where to deploy resources. Since this data skillfully informs us in which order to divert our attention, the customer will benefit and appreciate the results. Perhaps using this technique may give us an edge to our competition.

We now have completed the minimum or basic view of HOQ1, the Customer House. It provides us a good framework to combine two viewpoints from the customer's perspective: the VOCs and CTQs. Their VOCs include wants and needs, and the CTQs include their metrics of success, either imposed from the industry they serve or Key Performance Indicators chosen from their business. This nicely packed matrix of information will become the foundation for House of Quality 2 (HOQ2). In the next part of this book, Part 2, we will expand on the Design and R&D viewpoint to complete HOQ2 sometimes known as the Translation house. Later in Part 4 of the book, we will return to HOQ1 to expand it by adding more rooms and a roof. After all, if this table of data is called a House of Quality, it should look like a house.

Part 2

Design and R&D Viewpoint

In Part 1, we focused on the interaction of our company's commercial team with the customer, bringing an external viewpoint to us. Now in Part 2, we shift gears and explore how the internal interactions will determine the attributes and level of quality that our customer will be satisfied with. These business functions, such as design and R&D (research and development), don't normally interact directly with the customer, but their influence is significant because they help develop the product properties that the customer experiences. To know what it takes to achieve a positive customer reaction, we will use the customers' wants and needs captured from Part 1 which leads to identifying quality parameters. Later, we will sort out the most impactful ones. Finally, those external and internal metrics are organized and combined using the House of Quality 2.

Design and R&D Viewpoint

6

What Are the Product's Characteristics?

In previous chapters, the metrics that define the performance of our products that we supply to our customer were outlined. Now, we will expand on the quality aspects of our products from a fundamental level either from a chemical or physical perspective. The research and development (R&D) team will be pivotal in defining those technical features of the item being produced. In addition, a multifunctional team comprised of marketing, sales, with R&D will help shape the product's final features. Once the final product is well defined, it will be ready for production and made en masse.

6.1 WHAT DOES GOOD LOOK LIKE, METRICS OF SUCCESS FOR THE PRODUCT

To know what good looks like, we need to go back on how products are designed and created. There are many factors in designing a product such as customer feedback, scientific advances, technological capabilities, necessity, convenience, and many others. When these products go from a concept on a whiteboard to a tangible prototype, the R&D team is involved. The R&D team needs the help from marketing and sales to ensure that the product reflects the needs of the customers. As the new product goes through many different gyrations in the lab as part of the learning and discovery process, they outline the key product performance characteristics. These KPIs or Key Performance Indicators define what good looks like.

There are numerous methods on how to do product design and new product introductions. A proven method that has worked very well across multiple industries is using a stage-gate project structure. This approach involves breaking the product development cycle into multiple chunks or stages within the project. These stages are defined as major steps within the product development process and contain a list of expected requirements that need to be met. Once that stage has met those requirements, the project is ready for a review by a panel of key business decision makers from contrasting functions (commercial, finance, research, supply chain, purchasing, etc.) to provide a multifaceted viewpoint of the product and its final use. Figure 6.1 illustrates the Design for Six Sigma (DFSS) stage-gate process. The evaluation panel will determine one of three scenarios during the gate review: the product is feasible to proceed to the next stage, or it should be partly modified before moving on, or in rare cases, it can be abandoned altogether. This review in the process is referred to as the gate since it determines if the product goes forward or not. An example of this type of stage-gate process is the DFSS method of product development. The DFSS process is also called under its initials of the stages, DMADV (pronounced dee-mad-vee) which stand for Define, Measure, Analyze, Design, and Verify; expanding on this topic will take us beyond the scope we intend to cover in this book.

As mentioned earlier, the R&D has a pivotal role defining KPIs as metrics for success which can be leading or lagging indicators. A leading indicator is a metric that will predict or anticipate an outcome. An example of a leading indicator from Tubing Experts would be oven temperature and line speed. Keeping those two indicators under control maintains a consistent drying and curing of the painted tube. On the other hand, lagging indicators are measurements that confirm something that already has occurred, like checking the weight of the contents in a box. The process of putting the correct amount of product in the box already occurred, we are now verifying, after the fact, if the weight is correct. As these metrics are being defined, it would be advantageous to have leading indicators since they can help anticipate issues before they occur. Sometimes these

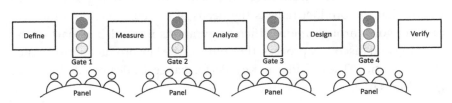

FIGURE 6.1
DFSS stage-gate process.

forward-looking indicators may not be available because they may be constrained by scientific limitations either physical or chemical.

When defining indicators, we need to know if these are metrics that can be measured in the production process. In order to do this, we need to ramp up the lab-made product to industrial quantities in production. The planning of the conditions on how to make the product from a lab scale to full size manufacturing is called scale-up. The R&D team will need to partner closely with operations to migrate from the lab to production. Scale-ups can be defined in two ways. One procedure will be to go in a single step from lab environments to industrial-sized equipment. The second form of scale-up may involve a two-step process. Step one is having a successful transfer from a lab scale to pilot plant. The second step is taking the learnings from the pilot scale to help make the product in the large capacity production plant. The pilot plant has the same equipment as the production plant; however, it is smaller in size and larger than the lab. This intermediate step has its advantages since it will not tie up precious production time to make trial runs and less trial test product may be wasted.

During the stage of product development, making inferior quality product is OK, in fact, it is what you want to do. Pushing your product to the extreme ranges of your metrics helps you understand the sensitivity of how certain process conditions may affect the Quality Control (QC) metrics. This sensitivity analysis will be very important later in House of Quality 3, the Manufacturing house.

6.1.1 Define QC Metrics

The R&D team will start defining the metrics that will determine the quality of the product. Defining quality in terms of specific metrics may help us know ahead of time if the product will perform satisfactorily or not. Because of these forward-looking measurements, these variables will later become Quality Control or QC metrics which will ensure that the customer receives a product that meets or exceeds their expectations. Some of these measurements may be done in real time during production and others need to be sampled and tested in a QC lab.

We learned in general terms how these KPIs are defined using lab tests, pilot runs, and scale-up trials. Let us put these concepts into practice using our fictitious company, Liquid Paint Specialists. The team has learned from their experimental runs to focus on five metrics: gel time, viscosity, surface appearance, gloss, and number of cracks.

Describing these KPIs can put it into context how they help become quality metrics. Starting with gel time, this value helps us understand if the paint is starting to thicken to a gel before it becomes cured. The procedure is done in the QC lab under a controlled temperature of 250°F. Therefore, the time it will take to thicken to a gel should occur at a specific range of time which in our case should happen in <60 seconds. If the product thickens within that time frame, we can expect the drying and cure time to occur within a predictable time at the customer as well. Therefore, we can use the gel time value as a leading indicator on how the product should perform at the customer. In other words, the paint should dry and cure on the tubes at the expected line speed at the customer's plant.

Viscosity measures the thickness of the liquid paint. The value is measured online during the making of the paint batch helping us understand if all formulation components are put in the right ratios since a slight deviation of these constituents can directly affect the viscosity values. As the previous metric, this QC value is a leading indicator.

Orange peel appearance, as the name suggests, is a textured surface that resembles the bumpy surface of the orange peel. The test is performed in the QC lab, and it makes use of a preparation panel which will be used for other tests. Optimizing the sampling preparation should be considered at this stage of product development while getting several QC measurements from one sample is a good head start. This reading is done visually and compared to a reference to determine good product versus bad quality product. It is important to note that this test is the first one to use the same panel in a nondestructive manner. Orange peel is a lagging indicator, and the next two metrics are also lagging measurements using the same panel.

Sixty-degree gloss is read in the lab using a handheld measurement device by using a beam of light to know how shiny or glossy the painted surface is. For the second time, we use the same panel originally used for the orange peel test. Since this panel was used only for reading the reflection of light, it can be used for our third and last test.

The last test measures the number of cracks which is very similar to the earlier metric used in House of Quality 1 (HOQ1) of crack rates. Back then, that metric was defined as 1 crack per 1,000 ft of tubes produced at the customer production plant. In this QC metric, we test the number of cracks on the same coated and cured panel for the third time. The R&D team determined that this sampling and measuring technique is a good representation of the full production batch. The panel is submitted to a destructive test method and cannot be used again since it is bent to stretch the paint without cracking. Our R&D team did a very good job in optimizing the sample preparation to make the most amount of measurements on that same panel before it was destroyed.

The QC variables are summarized in Table 6.1, highlighting the most important aspects of the product. These values will be combined with the Critical to Quality variables that were collected in HOQ1. We now have the two parts needed to start building House of Quality 2 (HOQ2) which will be detailed in Chapter 7. Now we are one step closer to reaching the factory floor. This concludes the gathering of the QC metrics.

TABLE 6.1

Quality Control Metrics and Specifications

Quality Control Metric	Specification	Indicator Type
Gel time @ 250°F	<60 seconds	Leading
Number of cracks	0–5	Lagging
Viscosity	Ford #4 cup (20–24 seconds)	Leading
Orange peel appearance	Pass = 1 no orange peel Fail = 0 orange peel present	Lagging
60° gloss	40–70 units	Lagging

7

Create House of Quality 2, the Translation House

The second House of Quality will be built in this chapter by using the Quality Control (QC) metrics from Chapter 6. How does this new house relate to the previous one? House of Quality 2 (HOQ2) is built by interconnecting elements of the previous House, House of Quality 1 (HOQ1) the Customer house. We will use the Critical to Quality (CTQ) metrics from HOQ1 defined in Chapter 5 and combine it with the recently defined QC metrics. The combination will help us translate the CTQs into QC metrics and that is where HOQ2 gets its name as the Translation house. The following sections will show how these parts are organized and assembled together.

7.1 ORGANIZE THE QC METRICS

In the previous chapter, we captured the QC metrics of our paint coating from our R&D team. Figure 7.1 shows the process of placing the QCs in HOQ2. These will be the first building blocks for creating the top room of HOQ2. This room has the QC metrics with their expected values and acceptable ranges. The QC details are highlighted in Table 7.1. In the table, the rightmost column indicates how the best results are attained either as reaching a target value or the direction for improvement.

These variables will be placed on the top room of HOQ2, using all the information gathered in Table 7.1. Once that data has been placed in the house, it should resemble Figure 7.2.

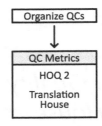

FIGURE 7.1
Organizing the QC metrics for HOQ2.

TABLE 7.1

QC Metrics for HOQ2

QC Metric	Specification	Metric Improvement Direction or Target
Gel time @ 250°F	<60 seconds	Lower is better
Number of cracks	0–5	Lower is better
Viscosity	Ford #4 cup (20–24 seconds)	Target
Orange peel appearance	Pass = 1 no orange peel	Target
	Fail = 0 orange peel present	
60° gloss	40–70 units	Target

House of Quality 2
Translation House

Metric improvement direction or target →		▼	▼	•	•	•	
Quality Control Metric, Target and Unit of Measure →		<60 Seconds	0-5	Ford #4 cup (20-24 sec)	Pass=1 no orange peel, Fail=0 orange peel present	40-70 Units	
Critical to Quality Metrics	Weight / Priority	Gel Time @ 250 F	Number of Cracks	Viscosity	Orange Peel Appearance	60-Degree Gloss	

FIGURE 7.2
QC targets and units of measure added to HOQ2.

7.2 COMBINE THE CTQ AND THE QC METRICS

We cascade from HOQ1 the CTQ metrics into HOQ2. The structure is like the first house we built, HOQ1, by placing the descending CTQs on the left side of the main room of HOQ2, as shown in Figure 7.3. This step is important to note since it connects the two houses together and flows the concepts captured from the customer side with our internal quality of the product. In other words, it connects the customer's expectations via the VOCs and CTQs with our R&D technical definitions given by the QC metrics.

We ranked the CTQs in HOQ1 for our example customer Tubing Experts back in Chapter 5. We then created a CTQ rankings Pareto chart that summarizes the effect that each CTQ had when combined with the impact of the VOC as shown in Figure 7.4. Later, we will construct the main room of HOQ2 once the top and side rooms are filled in as shown in Figure 7.5. Then, we will examine and evaluate each combination as we did for HOQ1 in Chapter 5.

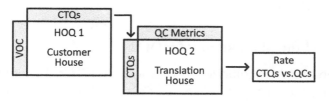

FIGURE 7.3
Cascading the CTQs from HOQ1 to HOQ2.

CTQ Rank	Critical to Quality Metrics	Relative Weight (% impact)
1	Tube integrity	18.6%
2	Holiday testing	18.1%
3	Consistency of cured film build	16.1%
4	Cure time	14.8%
5	Sticky tubes	14.8%
6	Plugged spray nozzles	13.1%
7	Crack rates	3.3%
8	Plugged filters	1.2%

FIGURE 7.4
CTQ rankings Pareto chart.

House of Quality 2
Translation House

Metric improvement direction or target →		▼	▼	•	•	•	
Quality Control Metric, Target and Unit of Measure →		<60 Seconds	0-5	Ford #4 cup (20-24 sec)	Pass=1 no orange peel, Fail=0 orange peel present	40-70 Units	
Critical to Quality Metrics	Weight / Priority	Gel Time @ 250 F	Number of Cracks	Viscosity	Orange Peel Appearance	60-Degree Gloss	
Crack rates	3.3%						
Cure time	14.8%						
Tube integrity	18.6%						
Plugged spray nozzles	13.1%						
Plugged filters	1.2%						
Sticky tubes	14.8%						
Consistency of cured film build	16.1%						
Holiday testing	18.1%						

FIGURE 7.5
CTQs and weights added to HOQ2.

7.2.1 Build the Main Room of HOQ2

We are now ready to combine the QCs with the CTQs. The order on how to interpret the relationship between QCs and CTQs is shown with the direction of the arrows in Figure 7.6.

The interpretation of the relationship between QCs and CTQs with the arrows is similar on how we did it in Chapter 5. We will use the same

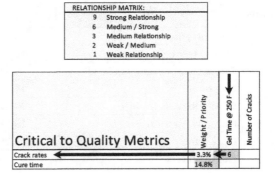

FIGURE 7.6
How to rate the relationship of a QC with a CTQ in HOQ2.

rating scales of the 9, 6, 3, 2, and 1 with strong relationship being a 9 and weaker ones down to 1. If there is no relationship, it will be kept empty. We will start with the leftmost column and going down the rows one by one to assess each CTQ. The calculations are the same as it was done for the first house.

7.3 RANK THE QC METRICS

7.3.1 House of Quality 2

The findings in HOQ2 are just as impactful as the first house. HOQ2 was combined with metrics that have been gathered from various sources and reveals interesting relationships (Figure 7.7). These interactions are expressed by looking at the ranking of the QC metrics either at the bottom of HOQ2 or at the Pareto chart in Figure 7.8. Gel time is the highest ranked QC metric with a value of 25.3% followed by two others that are ranked also near the 20% range: 60° gloss (22.6%) and number of cracks (19.4%).

The Translation house is now completed. This House of Quality combined the requirements from the customer side by using CTQs and adding

House of Quality 2
Translation House

Metric Improvement direction or target →		▼	▼	•	•	•	
Quality Control Metric, Target and Unit of Measure →		<60 Seconds	0-5	Ford #4 cup (20-24 sec)	Pass=1 no orange peel, Fail=0 orange peel present	40-70 Units	
Critical to Quality Metrics	Weight / Priority	Gel Time @ 250 F	Number of Cracks	Viscosity	Orange Peel Appearance	60-Degree Gloss	
Crack rates	3.3%	6	9	3	2	2	
Cure time	14.8%	9	3	6	3	6	
Tube integrity	18.6%						
Plugged spray nozzles	13.1%		1	1	9	3	
Plugged filters	1.2%		1		6		
Sticky tubes	14.8%	9	9			6	
Consistency of cured film build	16.1%	9	6	6	6	3	
Holiday testing	18.1%	3	3	6	2	9	
CALCULATED IMPORTANCE →		4.85	3.72	3.17	3.09	4.34	
Rank →		1	3	4	5	2	

FIGURE 7.7
Completed QCs and CTQs in HOQ2.

QCs Rank	Quality Control Metrics	Relative Weight (% impact)
1	Gel Time @ 250 F	25.3%
2	60-Degree Gloss	22.6%
3	Number of Cracks	19.4%
4	Viscosity	16.5%
5	Orange Peel Appearance	16.1%

FIGURE 7.8
QC rankings Pareto chart.

the R&D defined QC metrics. The matrix of weighted information from the two sources cited helps us understand those requirements in a balanced manner.

As mentioned before, the information will be used later to assess proactively the Quality metrics that can be used in operations. Just like how we cascaded HOQ1 into HOQ2, we will be doing a similar approach to build HOQ3 the Manufacturing house. This linkage is vital to create a seamless connectivity between what the customer wants and how we can make it in manufacturing. We are now one step closer of hearing the customer voice all the way to the factory floor.

Part 3

Operations Viewpoint

The focus in this part of this book will be the manufacturing of the product and sending it to the customer. Making use of the information gathered from previous chapters will help identify the needed metrics that will be used on the factory floor. As before, each variable will be prioritized and sorted. Later, all those variables will be combined to help construct the third and last House of Quality (HOQ). We need to ensure that those parameters in HOQ3 are monitored to maintain the expected outcome. Maintaining consistency will be done by using a Control Plan. All these topics will be detailed in Chapters 8–10.

8

Process Variables that Define Success on the Factory Floor

8.1 CONDITIONS FOR MANUFACTURING THE PRODUCT

The product finally left the manufacturing plant, making its journey to the customer. The work that went into making the product as it leaves production embodies many months of design, engineering, customers surveys, marketing research, etc. Once the customer receives the product, it hopefully meets their needs and, in the end, it is the customer who will be the ultimate arbiter to know how well it performed. Any deviation from their expectations will affect their opinion, positively or negatively (recall the Kano model, Chapter 2).

The manufacturing plant is comprised by two groups: the physical environment and the work environment. The physical environment is about the equipment and infrastructure of the plant where the work environment is the human factor or soft skills. If the physical environment is a reflection of technology, what is the work environment a reflection of? Ponder that thought for a moment. How does your company balance the work environment with the physical environment? Based on my observations, the work environment is a reflection of several aspects: management, connection with our customer, and relationship with our employees. Let's expand on these.

8.2 ARE WE WINNING OR ARE WE LOSING TODAY?

Since we are talking about manufacturing, do our manufacturing employees know how well we are performing today? Consider the following two scenarios. Each scenario highlights how a factory employee defines their performance.

> Scenario one: I walk to the warehouse and see one of our employees on a fork truck. He's loading a pallet of product on a truck for a customer. I shout to him, "Hey, are we winning or are we losing today?" He smiles, gives me a thumb up saying, "We're winning today, we're at 98%!" I nod and smile, knowing that 98% of the orders are fulfilled completely and shipped on time.
>
> Scenario two: I walk to the warehouse and see one of our employees on a fork truck. He's loading a pallet of product on a truck for a customer. I shout to him, "Hey, are we winning or are we losing today?" He looks befuddled, shrugging his shoulders, saying, "I don't know. I just work here." The fork truck driver only understands the product needs to be loaded on the truck for the customer. Nothing more. He is not interested in knowing if the company is winning or losing; he just wants to make it through the day.

In the first scenario, the fork truck driver knows his performance metric and what he is doing is important to the customer; he not only knows things are right qualitatively but he also knows it quantitatively. We are doing it 98% correct and that event captures the essence of this book's subtitle: *Hearing the Voice of the Customer on the Factory Floor*. As described in scenario one, this employee is listening and knowing how to measure what is important to the customer, even if he will never interact with the customer directly. Ninety-eight percent is our key metric of success. Recall how similar it is to what we learned in Chapter 3. Back then, the ultimate metric of success for our customer was mileage, and it was a value that meant so much to them; they used it as an incentive. The similarity here is that 98% (complete order and shipped on time) provides pride, success, and ultimately customer satisfaction. If you don't measure, how do you know if you are winning or losing?

8.2.1 Details Matter

In the previous section, we elaborated about metrics and how well employees are engaged with the product they provide to the customer. Here, we will expand on the soft skills, the work environment. I will define and expand on this topic by using the following narrative. Based on a first-hand experience from a business associate, the following incidence forever changed my view of the relationship of management and manufacturing employees.

> Vincent, an experienced mechanical engineer, was invited to a production facility to inspect the company's latest installation of coating technology. The industrial complex spanned several acres. Accompanied by the plant manager and lead engineer, Vincent toured the plant. He looked with detail on how the product traveled from unit operation to unit operation. By having multiple shadow boards and charts throughout the plant, it was apparent that Lean concepts were applied. The workstations followed 5s principles (Sort, Set in Order, Shine, Standardize, Sustain). Here and there, he did notice a few missing tools on the shadow boards; however, it didn't diminish the spirit of following Lean principles. Floors were marked to indicate where items should be placed and walkways clearly visible. Overall the factory floor was clean. About half way through the tour, Vincent asked to use the bathroom. The plant manager says, "We are far from the front office." Vincent replied that it would be okay for him to use the one right here, where the plant personnel goes. The two plant leaders looked at each other in disbelief and shrugged their shoulders and pointed to Vincent where to go. When Vincent went through the doorway, he passed through the locker rooms and right next to it was the bathroom. He had a sinking feeling going through those rooms. It seemed to him that he entered into another world, leaving behind the clean Lean environment he observed on the factory floor. Vincent stumbled through dingy rooms that were dimly lit, a few light fixtures hung empty, and fluorescent tubes buzzed, begging to be changed. The walls were filthy, the floors were sticky, and debris from many months accumulated in the corners. It's shameful to allow any person to go into these premises. After Vincent returned to the factory floor, he couldn't believe how can the plant manager allow this to happen. It occurred to him that it is a reflection of the management! It is a reflection of the front office, and ultimately a reflection of the company, representing how they view and treat their employees. Vincent pondered. What kind of products come

out of the factory floor? Do those production plant employees have pride making a high-quality product for their customer? He didn't think so. Hence, it was very difficult for him to focus and to continue the rest of the tour with a straight face.

This amazing story changed my entire perspective of how to treat employees. If the factory floor bathroom is not good enough for me to use, it is not good enough for anyone else. Change it! 5s it! It takes the concepts of Lean principles to the next level.

8.3 DEFINE PROCESS VARIABLES

Selecting Process Variables (PVs) can be overwhelming since there are so many measurements to take throughout the plant. We can measure just about anything in the production factory. To sort and identify the critical few, it can be done by a sub-team from engineering and R&D. These two departments can provide different perspectives. The research person will give weight on the principles of science and technology and the engineer will look at it from a practical and feasible approach. These viewpoints can be captured by brainstorming, organizing, and Pareto charting the most important ideas. The process of capturing these concepts has been described in detail in Chapter 2 when we looked at Value Proposition. Figure 8.1 highlights the steps needed to discover the critical few PVs.

Returning to our example of Liquid Paint Specialists, we went through the discovery and selection process by using brainstorming. The team broke down the manufacturing plant in different regions to define key areas of importance that may affect the making of paint. In addition, we involved experts from manufacturing, R&D, and engineering. The top four processes that we selected were raw materials (RMs), reactor, cooldown tank, and shipping.

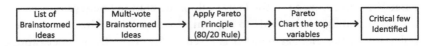

FIGURE 8.1
How to identify the critical few by using brainstorming.

Now let's define in more detail these four areas to determine the key PVs for each. Turning to the first selected area, RMs are added into the process in two forms: one is automatic, and the other is manual. The automated feeds are injected directly into the reactor. The manual added raws are pre-weighed and placed next to the reactor, so it can be added when needed. The PVs of interest for these RMs are target weight and correct ingredients.

The next area is the reactor which is the most vital unit operation of the manufacturing plant. It has the most amount of process control and instrumentation. Determining those critical few key PVs was a challenge since so many are available in this part of the process. The team settled with the following three variables: reactor temperature, reaction time, and agitator speed.

The third plant area was the cooldown tank. The cooldown tank helps quench the product made from the reactor; it stops the reaction from further advancement. This unit operation is all about taking heat away from the liquid product. Here the two key PVs selected are cooldown tank temperature and agitator speed.

The last area and most important to the customer is shipping. This is the last step before the product leaves our production facility and it is what the customer will experience. The product(s) must be shipped correctly to them and the order must contain all the items that they requested. The appropriate metric from production will be a complete order and shipped on time. Remember earlier, the smiling fork truck driver saying we are winning today! He knew that 98% was a reflection about this metric.

Consider the following analogy. Instead of making paint, let's bake a cake. The RMs are the cake ingredients. The reactor is the kitchen oven. Cooldown is the room temperature. Shipping is equivalent of making the cake on time and transporting it to the event. Each PV is important and will predict that a cake will fulfill the expectations of the guests. Since these variables predict whether the outcome is acceptable or not, all chosen PVs are considered leading indicators.

All PVs for Liquid Paint Specialists are summarized in Table 8.1 with the desired ranges for each one. These PVs will be combined with the Quality Control metrics from House of Quality 2 (HOQ2). The last step before moving into building House of Quality 3 (HOQ3), which we will do next in Chapter 9.

TABLE 8.1

Process Variables Metrics and Specifications

PVs Metric	Specification	Indicator Type
Manually added RMs	Target amount and type (lb)	Leading
Automatically added RMs	Target amount and type (lb)	Leading
Reactor temperature	255–285°F	Leading
Reaction time in reactor	110–130 minutes	Leading
Reactor agitator speed	45 rpm	Leading
Cooldown tank temperature	Cool to below 80°F	Leading
Cooldown tank agitator speed	85 rpm	Leading
Complete order and shipped on time	>95%	Leading

9

Create House of Quality 3, the Manufacturing House

In this chapter, we are at the final stretch of building the third and last House of Quality. This house focuses on the production of the finished product, and it is appropriately called the Manufacturing house. Here, the employees on the factory floor make the product that our customers will experience.

9.1 ORGANIZE THE PROCESS VARIABLES

In the last chapter, Process Variables (PVs) were defined with a core team of experts from manufacturing, research and development (R&D), and engineering. Figure 9.1 shows the process of placing the PVs in House of Quality 3 (HOQ3). These PVs are the components for creating the top room of HOQ3. This room has the PV metrics with their expected values and acceptable ranges. The PV details are highlighted in Table 9.1. The rightmost column indicates how the best results are attained either by reaching a target value or direction for improvement.

The PVs will be placed on the top room of HOQ3. These will use all the information gathered in Table 9.1. Once that data have been placed in the house, it should resemble Figure 9.2.

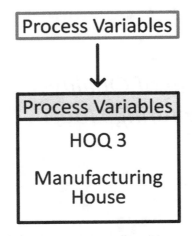

FIGURE 9.1
Organizing the PVs for HOQ3.

TABLE 9.1

Process Variables Metrics for HOQ3

PVs Metric	Specification	Metric Improvement Direction or Target
Manually added RMs	Target amount and type (lb)	Target
Automatically added RMs	Target amount and type (lb)	Target
Reactor temperature	255–285°F	Target
Reaction time in reactor	110–130 minutes	Target
Reactor agitator speed	45 rpm	Target
Cooldown tank temperature	Cool to below 80°F	Lower is better
Cooldown tank agitator speed	85 rpm	Target
Complete order and shipped on time	>95%	Higher is better

9.2 COMBINE THE QC METRICS AND THE PROCESS VARIABLES

As we did before for House of Quality 2 (HOQ2), we will be cascading the HOQ2 Quality Control (QC) metrics into HOQ3. The structure is like the previous houses we built. We will be placing the QC metrics on the left side of the main room of HOQ3, as shown in Figure 9.3. Important to note, this last step connects the three houses together, starting with the

House of Quality 3
Manufacturing House

Metric improvement direction or target →		•	•	•	•	•	▼	•	▲	
Process Variables Target and Unit of Measure →		Target Amount and Type (lb)	Target Amount and Type (lb)	255-285 (°F)	110 - 130 (min)	45 (RPM)	Cool to below 80 (°F)	85 (RPM)	>95%	
Quality Control Metric	Weight / Priority	Manually added RMs	Automatically added RMs	Reactor Temperature	Reaction time in reactor	Reactor agitator speed	Cooldown tank temperature	Cooldown tank agitator speed	Complete order and shipped on time	

FIGURE 9.2

PVs targets and units of measure added to HOQ3.

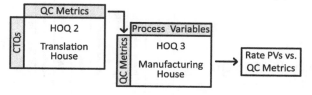

FIGURE 9.3

Cascading the QC metrics and weights from HOQ2 into HOQ3.

concepts captured externally from the customer in HOQ1 and flowing into HOQ3 with our PVs.

In Figure 9.4, we ranked the QCs in HOQ2 for our fictitious company, Liquid Paint Specialists, back in Chapter 7. Next, we start filling the top room in HOQ3 (Figure 9.5). Later, we will examine and evaluate each combination as we did for HOQ2 in Chapter 7.

9.2.1 Build the Main Room of HOQ3

We are now ready to combine the PVs with the QCs. The order to interpret the relationship between PVs and QCs is depicted with the direction of the arrows shown in Figure 9.6.

QCs Rank	Quality Control Metrics	Relative Weight (% impact)
1	Gel Time @ 250 F	25.3%
2	60-Degree Gloss	22.6%
3	Number of Cracks	19.4%
4	Viscosity	16.5%
5	Orange Peel Appearance	16.1%

FIGURE 9.4
QC rankings Pareto chart.

House of Quality 3
Manufacturing House

Metric Improvement direction or target →	•	•	•	•	•	▼	•	▲	
Process Variables Target and Unit of Measure →	Target Amount and Type (lb)	Target Amount and Type (lb)	255-285 (°F)	110 - 130 (min)	45 (RPM)	Cool to below 80 (°F)	85 (RPM)	>95%	

Quality Control Metric	Weight / Priority	Manually added RMs	Automatically added RMs	Reactor Temperature	Reaction time in reactor	Reactor agitator speed	Cooldown tank temperature	Cooldown tank agitator speed	Complete order and shipped on time	
Gel Time @ 250 F	25.3%									
Number of Cracks	19.4%									
Viscosity	16.5%									
Orange Peel Appearance	16.1%									
60-Degree Gloss	22.6%									

FIGURE 9.5
QCs and weights added to HOQ3.

The interpretation of the relationship between PVs and QC metrics with the arrows is similar to the way we did in Chapters 5 and 7. We will use the same rating scales of the 9, 6, 3, 2, and 1, with a strong relationship being a 9 and weaker ones down to 1. If there is no relationship, it will be kept empty. We will start with the leftmost column and going down the rows one by one to assess each PV; the completed main room should resemble Figure 9.7. The calculations are the same as it was done for HOQ1 in Chapter 5.

RELATIONSHIP MATRIX:	
9	Strong Relationship
6	Medium / Strong
3	Medium Relationship
2	Weak / Medium
1	Weak Relationship

Quality Control Metric	Weight / Priority	Manually added RMs	Automatically added RMs
Gel Time @ 250 F	◄— 25.3% ◄	9	
Number of Cracks	19.4%		

FIGURE 9.6
How to rate the relationship of a PV with a QC in HOQ3.

House of Quality 3
Manufacturing House

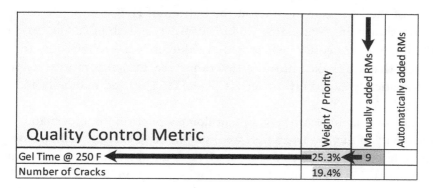

Quality Control Metric	Weight / Priority	Manually added RMs	Automatically added RMs	Reactor Temperature 255-285 (°F)	Reaction time in reactor 110 - 130 (min)	Reactor agitator speed 45 (RPM)	Cooldown tank temperature Cool to below 80 (°F)	Cooldown tank agitator speed 85 (RPM)	Complete order and shipped on time >95%	
Metric improvement direction or target →		•	•	•	•	•	▼	•	▲	
Gel Time @ 250 F	25.3%	9	9	9	6	3	3	3	9	
Number of Cracks	19.4%	9	9	9	9	9	6	6	9	
Viscosity	16.5%	9	9	9	9	6	9	9	9	
Orange Peel Appearance	16.1%	6	9	6	6	6	3	3	9	
60-Degree Gloss	22.6%	6	6	9	6	3			9	
CALCULATED IMPORTANCE →		7.84	8.32	8.52	7.08	5.14	3.89	3.89	9	
Rank →		4	3	2	5	6	7	8	1	

FIGURE 9.7
Completed PVs and QCs in HOQ3.

9.3 RANK THE PROCESS VARIABLES

9.3.1 House of Quality 3

The findings in HOQ3 are impactful like the other two houses but with a more focused view of production. These interactions express the rankings of the PVs metrics either at the bottom of HOQ3 or at the Pareto chart shown in Figure 9.8. Complete order and shipped on time is the highest ranked PV metric with a value of 16.8% followed by three others that are ranked near the 15% range: reactor temperature (15.9%), automatically added raw materials (RMs) (15.5%), and manually added RMs (14.6%).

Back in Chapter 6, we spoke about doing a pilot run to understand the sensitivity of the PVs when they were submitted to extreme values. Doing those tests proved valuable since it gives us an operating window in the manufacturing plant and still make high-quality product. For example, the reactor temperature can operate within a 30° range; it can be as low as 255°F and as high as 285°F. It is also the second most important ranked variable in our Pareto chart.

The manufacturing house is now complete. This house combined QC metrics from R&D with the production PVs. The matrix of weighted information in the main room helps us understand, in a balance manner, those requirements. Since we finally reached the factory floor with the HOQ3, the linkage is complete between what the customer wants

PV Rank	Process Variables	Relative Weight (% impact)
1	Complete order and shipped on time	16.8%
2	Reactor Temperature	15.9%
3	Automatically added RMs	15.5%
4	Manually added RMs	14.6%
5	Reaction time in reactor	13.2%
6	Reactor agitator speed	9.6%
7	Cooldown tank temperature	7.3%
8	Cooldown tank agitator speed	7.3%

FIGURE 9.8
PVs rankings Pareto chart.

and how we can manufacture it. Now, we can hear the customer voice all the way to the factory floor, and that is a major milestone.

How do we maintain this success? We need to ensure we have a way of identifying the controls and sustain them. We will explore the Control Plan in the next chapter.

10

Create the Control Plan

The results from House of Quality 3 (HOQ3) are the foundation in developing a Control Plan. This last house focuses on key Process Variables (PVs) that aid the manufacturing of high-quality product. Moreover, all those manufacturing metrics are leading indicators, ensuring a suitable product for our customer. Identifying PVs is not enough, and we need more definitions on how to control and maintain those operating ranges from HOQ3. The outcome of this chapter is to manufacture a consistent predictable quality product, in other words, sustain the gains.

10.1 SUSTAIN THE GAINS

What happens if the variable is not within the defined values? How much variation is acceptable before a change is needed? The key PVs, as defined in Chapter 8, need to be maintained at a target value within specified ranges. We learned about the sensitivity of the PVs during the scale-up process. There, we not only learned which variables are impactful to product quality but also how much change affects the quality of the product. During the scale-up process, we gathered data which helped us understand the relationships and interactions of the PVs with the Quality Control (QC) metrics. Those building blocks of knowledge will help us put together the pieces needed to start making the Control Plan and sustain the PVs at or near their targets.

The Control Plan is a document that captures the acceptable ranges of operating parameters during the manufacturing of the product, and also it helps adjust that PV back to the acceptable range. The Control Plan is made up of five information parts: process step, measuring type,

Process	Measurement Type	Process Variable	Measurement	Reaction Plan

FIGURE 10.1
Parts of the Control Plan.

PV, measurement information, and reaction plan. Figure 10.1 shows those parts.

The boxes indicate the location where these variables are in the manufacturing plant, how these are measured, and what to do if these are not within an acceptable range. The expanded parts are shown in Figure 10.2.

To understand how these expanded parts work, we will use a PV from Liquid Paint Specialists. This example becomes the source for developing a complete Control Plan with a reaction plan. The eight PVs identified from the Pareto chart in HOQ3 (Figure 10.3) have the variables sorted from the most important to least and will be used to create the Control Plan.

The best way to populate the Liquid Paint Specialist Control Plan document is filled out one part at a time starting with Process. The following figures (10.1 through 10.4) show step-by-step how the highest ranked PV (complete order and in time) is filled out.

We now start to fill the Control Plan. **Process** has two sub-parts regarding manufacturing location and measurement type. The first sub-part is **Process Step Metric** which is the measured PV (complete order and shipped on time). The **Unit Operation** is where the process step metric is located; in this case, it is in the shipping area. The **Measurement Type** is shown as an **Output** variable and the unit **Type** is % (percent). The **Process Variable LSL** (Lower Specification Limit) is the lowest acceptable value while still making high-quality product. In our current example, we chose 95%. Going below the 95% LSL triggers the reaction plan on how to rectify this issue (described later in this section). **Target** is the desired value we are striving to obtain, typically the midpoint value between the LSL and the USL (Upper Specification Limit). The target here is 97.5%. The **USL** for production is 100%, defining the maximum value we can have before triggering the reaction plan. In this case, 100% complete order and the order to be 100% on time cannot go beyond those values which

Process					Measurement Type	Process Variable				Measurement		Reaction Plan	
Process Step Metric	Unit Operation, Machine Name	Input	Output	Type	LSL (Production)	Target	USL (Production)	Method	Frequency	Current Control Method	Reaction Plan		

FIGURE 10.2
Parts of the Control Plan with details.

PV Rank	Process Variables	Relative Weight (% impact)
1	Complete order and shipped on time	16.8%
2	Reactor Temperature	15.9%
3	Automatically added RMs	15.5%
4	Manually added RMs	14.6%
5	Reaction time in reactor	13.2%
6	Reactor agitator speed	9.6%
7	Cooldown tank temperature	7.3%
8	Cooldown tank agitator speed	7.3%

FIGURE 10.3
PVs rankings Pareto chart.

Process Control Plan for Liquid Paint Specialists										
Process		Measurement Type			Process Variable			Measurement		Current Control Method	Reaction Plan
Process Step Metric	Unit Operation, Machine Name	Input	Output	Type	LSL (Production)	Target	USL (Production)	Method	Frequency		
Complete order and shipped on time	Shipping		yes	%	95	97.5	100	count	each order	Verify that each purchase order is completely fulfilled and shipped on time.	**Order not completely fulfilled:** determine why line item is missing and start investigation process. **Order not shipped on time:** determine why order has been delayed and start investigation process.

FIGURE 10.4
Control Plan with one PV and its reaction plan.

defines a boundary. Therefore, this PV is allowed to operate between the range of 95% and 100%. Anything below 95%, the reaction plan is triggered. It is important to note that these are production specifications and not customer specifications. This difference is very important and will be expanded in more detail in the next section.

The **Measurement Method** is how each PV is taken, and the **Frequency** defines how often the measurement is done. In our example, each purchase order is counted. In the **Reaction Plan**, the **Current Control Method** explains how the PV is captured: verify that each purchase order is completely fulfilled and shipped on time. If the value is not within the stated LSL and USL, the **Reaction Plan** is now triggered. This contingency strategy returns the PV to the normal operating range which has been developed during scale-up. The details of the **Reaction Plan** are on the far right column, and they explain, in our example, how to react when the value is not above the 95% range triggering an investigation.

The remaining PVs in the Control Plan with their respective reaction plans are shown in Figure 10.5. The details shown in the Control Plan figure follows the same logic as explained in the previous section.

10.1.1 Are These Customer Specifications or Production Specifications?

Measurements that are taken internally in the manufacturing process can sometimes be passed onto the customer. The customer notices that the values did not match the expected target, becoming concerned. The confusion may be caused by subtle differences on the way the producer measures internal product and how the customer measures it. Since we are evaluating the same product, the two observations may have different interpretations. Looking back at HOQ3, the PVs affect the manufacturing conditions and they are tested using the QC metrics. Some of those QC metrics are strictly internal production metrics, and they anticipate, as a leading indicator should do, how the product may perform at the customer. Providing to the customer, our internal QC metrics may cause contradictory results. For example, a company supplies oil at a certain viscosity that they measure internally. The customer receiving the oil also measures the viscosity using their own methods and instruments. When the customer saw the internal values of viscosity from the supplier to be lower than the one they measure, they rejected it immediately. However, the product was never out of spec on viscosity. They both were not using the same viscosity

	Process		Measurement Type			Process Variable			Measurement			
Process Control Plan for Liquid Paint Specialists												
Process Step Metric	Unit Operation, Machine Name	Input	Output	Type	LSL (Production)	Target	USL (Production)	Method	Frequency	Current Control Method	Reaction Plan
Complete order and shipped on time	Shipping		yes	%	95	97.5	100	count	each order	Verify that each purchase order is completely fulfilled and shipped on time.	**Order not completely fulfilled:** determine why line item is missing and start investigation process. **Order not shipped on time:** determine why order has been delayed and start investigation process.
Reactor Temperature	Reactor	yes		°F	255	270	285	gauge	each batch	Capture each batch to verify within production specs.	Adjust setpoint to compensate deviation. Repeat this process twice. If after two adjustment temp is not to target, shutdown and start investigation process.
Automatically added RMs	Raw materials	yes		lb	N/A	Correct target amount	N/A	flow meter, bar code	each RM	Capture each batch to verify within production specs.	If metered amount is greater that 1% from target, shutdown and start investigation process.
Manually added RMs	Raw materials	yes		lb	N/A	Correct target amount	N/A	scales, bar code	each RM	Capture each batch to verify within production specs.	If metered amount is greater that 1% from target, shutdown and start investigation process.
Reaction time in reactor	Reactor		yes	min	110	120	130	timer	each batch	Capture each batch to verify within production specs.	Ensure that the metered amount of RMs are within 1% target. If all RMs are within 1% of target and reaction time is beyond the LSL and USL, shutdown and start investigation process.
Reactor agitator speed	Reactor	yes		RPM	N/A	45	N/A	gauge	each batch	Capture each batch to verify within production specs.	Adjust setpoint to compensate deviation. Repeat this process twice. If after two adjustments RPM is not to target, shutdown and start investigation process.
Cooldown tank temperature	Cooldown tank		yes	°F	ambient	80	N/A	gauge	each batch	Capture each batch to verify within production specs.	Adjust setpoint to compensate deviation. Repeat this process twice. If after two adjustment temp is not to target, shutdown and start investigation process.
Cooldown tank agitator speed	Cooldown tank	yes		RPM	N/A	85	N/A	gauge	each batch	Capture each batch to verify within production specs.	Adjust setpoint to compensate deviation. Repeat this process twice. If after two adjustments RPM is not to target, shutdown and start investigation process.

FIGURE 10.5

Control Plan with all PVs and reaction plan.

instrument and method of measurement. These metrics were not equal and led to confusion of whether the oil was out of spec or not. It is important to identify clearly which metrics are for internal use and which are shared externally. In addition, if the viscosity metric is shared externally and the customer would like to double check the values with their own testing, make sure that the same procedure and instrument is communicated to the customer, ensuring consistency between their measurement values and the suppliers.

10.2 CONTROL PLAN REVISIONS AND TRAINING

The Control Plan is a living document. It should not be viewed as something done once and shelved. The document must be reviewed to ensure it captures the current state of the process. When process changes are considered, proper management of change procedures should be applied, and a line item needs to be added to include updating the Control Plan. Another simple approach would be to have an annual review to capture subtle changes of the process or other dependent procedures.

The Control Plan can also be the foundation for training new employees on how to operate the different unit operations and how to react when the PVs are not operating within the recommended ranges. Consider refresher training sessions for employees as this approach will force the document to be reviewed annually. This approach will maximize the effort in a threefold manner, not only having employees using a consistent method of operating the process, but also training employees on a periodic basis and finally helping to keep the documentation current.

We have reached the end of the Control Plan process and documentation. Hopefully, using the topics covered in this chapter may aid you in sustaining the gains.

Part 4

All Together Now, Threading the Needle

We've reached the part of this book where we will thread all the parts together and form a comprehensive fabric of success. Thanks for staying with me during this time. So far, I explained how to connect the Voice of the Customer to the three business functions so they can work as one cohesive and unified team. These functions are commercial (sales and marketing), research and development (product properties and services), and operations or manufacturing (product quality). We have systematically threaded that customer's voice through the Houses of Quality (HOQs) in a detailed and methodical approach. The techniques discussed in the past few chapters should work for most of you. It could be that your process or product will not fit exactly those steps as described. How can we adapt this new thinking to your situation? You also may ask: are three houses required every time? Can those HOQs be modified? What if I have a simple product or a more complex product? Does the HOQ apply to those as well? Together we will answer those questions and go through the appropriate actions needed. Maybe, by exploring the methods and concepts used in the next few chapters, you may formulate the answers to those questions.

Part I

All Together Now
Threading the Needle

11

Freedom within a Framework

Framework. It sounds so rigid. It portrays an image of sturdiness, inflexibility, and immovability. Let's reimagine a framework to be like an outer edge such as a fence around a property. The fence provides you boundaries and limits your space, providing safety and security. It can be a property limit, or a safety concern from the nearby cliff, or a myriad of other issues. In addition, within that framework, we have freedom: freedom within a framework. That freedom allows us to build a home within the fence, or keep the farm animals reigned in, or build a community park for the neighborhood. The ideas are limitless. When we apply the concept of freedom within a framework with the Houses of Quality (HOQs), we will discover a different approach of connecting the HOQ information in a more streamlined manner called the House of Quality flow down.

11.1 PREDICTABLE RESULTS AND FRAMEWORK

We described earlier of a framework to be an edge or perimeter. Another way to think of a framework is that it can be used as a backbone, something that helps maintain things together and provides a desired outcome. A single-family home built from a wooden frame supports floors, interior walls, exterior features, and a roof. A framework can also be made from steel, and those metal beams create a tall skyscraper. Those backbones or supporting structures are exactly what we have made with the HOQs. We already experienced in previous chapters the framework of three houses: HOQ1, the Customer house; HOQ2, the Translation house; and HOQ3, the Manufacturing house. Each one has its attributes or metrics, and those values will change depending on the product you will build.

Let's understand the relationship between framework and results. The two concepts of framework and results may sound unrelated. However, connecting the two will reveal a much-needed outcome to make the Voice of the Customer (VOC) heard throughout the organization all the way to the factory floor.

The first concept, framework, is about the use of a structured method like the HOQs or Standard Operating Procedures (SOPs). SOPs detail how to perform a task. These tasks can be a simple procedure such as affixing a sticker to a side panel, or as complex as the entire process of making a product. We can expand to what degree these outcomes can be *Yes: With framework* or *No: Without framework*.

The second concept is about results which can be either expectations or outcomes delivered to our customers. In our case of making products, these results manifest themselves as specifications such as on time delivery. Instead of simply saying results, let's expand the definition of results to include predictability. These also will have two outcomes *Yes: Predictable Results* or *No: Unpredictable Results*. Combining the two different values of framework with the two distinct types of results leads to four outcomes. Two are not quantifiable, and therefore, these are not practical. The other two are quantifiable, and only one is the desired combination we want. Let's see how these combinations fair out.

We will now show graphically how all these combinations align on a 2 × 2 matrix as shown in Figure 11.1. The dotted line boxes are to ones that are not practical. These are Predictable Results without framework and Unpredictable Results with a framework. One will not follow a pattern or structure, and the other, the customer, will not receive a product with consistent results. The product outcomes and the workplace may feel chaotic.

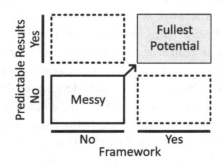

FIGURE 11.1
Predictable results and framework.

Therefore, we will not even elaborate these two options. The next two combinations make better sense, and we will describe in detail the relationships of framework with predictable results.

11.1.1 The First Quantifiable Combination: Unpredictable Results without Framework

The combination of unpredictable results and without using a framework leads to a **Messy** process. This outcome is like commanding a ship without a rudder and, on top of that, without a map to know precisely where your destination is. How does that look like in the workplace? If you don't have a framework, each person will make their own. Some people are well organized and will create a structure for themselves. Others may just wing it and try different approaches every time either consciously or unconsciously. Some will try different methods based on their mood. Perhaps, today is "good feeling day" and things go well, and the next day it's a "bad feeling day" becoming a difficult workday. It varies from day to day and from product to product making unpredictable results. The workplace, as the name of this combination implies, looks haphazard and disorganized; it is the most stressful.

Who are the ones in the **Messy** combination? They are the ones to go without a framework because they want fast results and lack patience to go slow to go fast. They are the ones that jump right into a "project" and want immediate results, showing visible progress. Those immediate results are just an illusion, and perhaps they reinvent the proverbial wheel by redoing their process in a needless manner, all because there isn't a framework in place. This type of worker just knows how to consistently figure it out to deliver the desired results, working and reworking parts of the project until it is done just right. This process is not cheap since it is not a straightforward approach. Using Lean terminology, this method has a lot of waste and rework since the process isn't streamlined. The factory may seem artificially busy. I once heard a very good statement which will apply well under these conditions: "Hey George, why don't you sharpen your axe. It is completely blunt." George replies, "I don't have time for that. I'm too busy chopping down the tree." This story exemplifies the **Messy** workplace by not taking the time to understand the fundamentals and prepare for the situation. When it comes down to executing the process, we need to pause and take time to think. Pausing and evaluating the tool made us think about sharpening the axe. A sharpened tool chops down a tree much faster; by taking the time to think, we use more brain power and less muscle power to stay busy longer with a blunt axe.

Here's another perspective about people wanting immediate results. How many of us have bought a new appliance, or a toy, assembled it, and it didn't work? After several frustrating attempts, we give up and contact customer service. The friendly voice on the phone asks: did you follow the steps outlined in the manual? When this happened to me, I chuckled knowing that I did not read the manual first. Instead, the excitement of the moment led me to just wing it and put the item together as I believed it should fit. I didn't follow the framework of reading the manual.

We've all met people that feel uneasy having boundaries or limits. Some of them absolutely cannot function with a framework. I met researchers who felt that they cannot be creative under the self-imposed mental constraints of a framework. They told me repeatedly that it will limit their creativity. My rebuttal was *freedom within a framework* is not *framework to stifle freedom*. Let me illustrate this point. Instead of defining framework to be a boundary, consider it to be a blank canvas. Clean, fresh, ready to receive the paint of a creative mind of an artist. The canvas is a framework: it has an edge. Without it, many masterpieces would have not been created!

11.1.2 The Second Quantifiable Combination: Predictable Results with Framework

What will be the opposite of **Messy**? **Fullest Potential**. Using consistently a framework or structured approach will help you deliver predictable results, providing an easily followed line of sight which clearly defines the process not only for yourself but for others as well. This combination is like a GPS map helping you to stay on course, so you can reach the desired destination. For example, an SOP will outline the steps on how to do a specific job or task. An SOP provides consistency on how to do the described task, so all employees follow it the same way. The workplace feels organized and stable. Employees are content, conveying a sense of security, bringing them to their **Fullest Potential**.

A summary of the different frameworks is shown in Figure 11.1 along with their predictable results. The desired path of success is to migrate from the **Messy** quadrant to the **Fullest Potential** quadrant. After reviewing the last few examples, where do you see yourself? Are you surprised?

11.1.3 An Example: Let's Have a Party

I am having a party this weekend at my home. I invited friends and family. Before the weekend arrives, I need to plan for the event. I go to the supermarket to pick up some meats, vegetables, drinks, and desserts. The supermarket has a framework organized nicely for me to get my items. Everything is neatly displayed and put into shelves. The isles are labeled with related items placed near each other. Considering what meats to buy, I can choose beef, lamb, pork, chicken, etc.; it can be a steak, a roast, ribs, or ground meat. In addition, I can get grass-fed or lean, bulk or pre-sliced, premade, or pre-cooked, and I can even have it catered and delivered to my home. These options allow me to get all those degrees of freedoms within the framework of food-related items. Because of that successful framework, it allows me to go to other supermarkets and pretty much find those items in the same manner because that structure is common among different supermarkets across town, across the country, and even across the world. We are accustomed of that arrangement, so that framework provides convenience.

Now the scalability of the supermarket framework also brings some inconveniences. I cannot buy whatever item I want, nor can I pay whatever price I want. I will not be able to go into a supermarket and ask for a brand new car or buy a CNC machine. I can't do that; that is the limitation of that framework of grocery items.

As you may have figured out, these freedoms within a framework are all around us. Cities exhibit this structure with city limits and a grid of streets, parcels of land with homes, and libraries with organized information by subject. The pattern of freedom within a framework repeats itself in institutions, jobs, positions within a company, even this book you are now reading. Regarding your situation, how can you rethink in this manner the area of influence you have? This is the way how a change agent thinks: influencing with new concepts, providing examples, and adapting it to your work area, your reality.

11.2 COMPLETE THE HOUSES OF QUALITY

We developed the HOQs in earlier chapters by connecting loosely the HOQs, cascading the values from one house to the next. In doing so, it created a connectivity from the VOC to the Manufacturing floor.

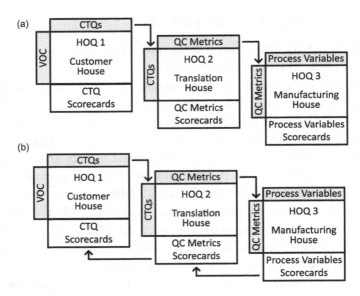

FIGURE 11.2
(a) Three HOQs connected. (b) Three HOQs connected with scorecard flow up.

Linking each house leads us to the full view depicted in Figure 11.2a, clarifying that the flow is fluid and seamless through the different house metrics, ensuring product quality and customer satisfaction.

Constructed earlier from Chapters 5 to 9, we moved the metrics from HOQ1 to HOQ2 and finally to HOQ3. The down arrows in Figure 11.2a show the direction of the cascading effects of the metrics from one house to the next. Just as important, the scorecards on the bottom of each HOQ summarize the results of each house. These scorecards are also connected between the houses as exemplified in Figure 11.2b with the up arrows.

Starting from the third HOQ, we see the upward connectivity of the manufacturing scorecard metrics all the way to the customer scorecard. Now, that fluid connectivity goes both ways from the customer to the factory floor and the factory floor back to the customer.

11.3 HEARING THE CUSTOMER AT THE FACTORY FLOOR

The metrics that flow from house to house can also create a streamlined version of all the houses as shown in Figure 11.3. Only the variables that appear on the scorecard are placed in the HOQ flow down.

House of Quality flow down			
Customer House HOQ1		**Translation House, HOQ2**	**Manufacturing House, HOQ3**
What does the customer say they want?	Critical to Quality for the customer's needs (how does the customer determine satisfaction?)	How will we make sure we meet the customers' requirements (CTQs)? (what must the product do to meet the CTQs?)	How will we <u>control the</u> manufacturing <u>process</u> to ensure we meet the QC metrics?
Voice of Customer	**Critical to Quality**	**Quality Control Metric**	**Process Variables**
Product is within specs Our product improves your productivity Mileage made today Even coating thickness Appearance	Crack rates Cure time Tube integrity Plugged spray nozzles Plugged filters Sticky tubes Consistency of cured film build Holiday testing	Gel Time @ 250 F Number of Cracks Viscosity Orange Peel Appearance 60-Degree Gloss	Complete order and shipped on time Reactor Temperature Automatically added RMs Manually added RMs Reaction time in reactor Reactor agitator speed Cooldown tank temperature Cooldown tank agitator speed

FIGURE 11.3
HOQ flow down.

This arrangement has one exception with the first HOQ. The VOC metric in HOQ1 does not have a scorecard, and it is placed together with the Critical to Quality (CTQ) in the flow down. The top row of the flow down helps identify from which house the attribute comes from, making the linkage easier to interpret. In addition, key questions help summarize the intent of each HOQ. The first house targets customer needs with the VOC metrics. The question asked for HOQ1 is: What does the customer say they want? The second question on that same HOQ1 is related to CTQ: How does the customer determine satisfaction? Moving along to the next column for HOQ2, the questions will be asked from two different perspectives. The first inquiry is from the customer's needs perspective. How will we make sure we meet the customers' requirements (CTQs)? The second question is looking at it from the product perspective. What must the product do to meet the CTQs? Finally, in the Manufacturing House, HOQ3, the last question is related to manufacturing conditions to ensure a quality product for the customer. How will we control the manufacturing process to ensure we meet the Quality Control (QC) metrics?

By completing the metrics in this manner, it provides a simple clean look of all variables from left to right.

Another use of the HOQ flow down can be as a starting point to build the original HOQs as we did in earlier chapters. Some people use it as a list to identify the variables of interest for making the HOQs. Later, they will rearrange the metrics by placing those in the standard form as we have done in previous chapters. Figure 11.4 shows how to build HOQ2 using information from the HOQ flow down.

House of Quality flow down			
Customer House HOQ1		**Translation House, HOQ2**	**Manufacturing House, HOQ3**
What does the customer say they want?	Critical to Quality for the customer's needs (how does the customer determine satisfaction?)	How will we make sure we meet the customers' requirements (CTQs)? (what must the product do to meet the CTQs?)	How will we **control the** manufacturing **process** to ensure we meet the QC metrics?
Voice of Customer	**Critical to Quality**	**Quality Control Metric**	**Process Variables**
Product is within specs Our product improves your productivity Mileage made today Even coating thickness Appearance	Crack rates Cure time Tube integrity Plugged spray nozzles Plugged filters Sticky tubes Consistency of cured film build Holiday testing	Gel Time @ 250 F Number of Cracks Viscosity Orange Peel Appearance 60-Degree Gloss	Complete order and shipped on time Reactor Temperature Automatically added RMs Manually added RMs Reaction time in reactor Reactor agitator speed Cooldown tank temperature Cooldown tank agitator speed

House of Quality 2
Translation House

Metric improvement direction or target →

Quality Control Metric, Target and Unit of Measure →

Critical to Quality Metrics	Weight / Priority	Gel Time @ 250 F	Number of Cracks	Viscosity	Orange Peel Appearance	60-Degree Gloss	
Crack rates	3.3%						
Cure time	14.8%						
Tube integrity	18.6%						
Plugged spray nozzles	13.1%						
Plugged filters	1.2%						
Sticky tubes	14.8%						
Consistency of cured film build	16.1%						
Holiday testing	18.1%						

FIGURE 11.4
Using HOQ flow down to build a HOQ.

11.3.1 Who Connects Each HOQ?

The HOQ flow down shows the connectivity flowing from left to right and right to left as shown in Figure 11.3. We also have shown in Figure 11.2b the expanded connectivity cascades from house to house and upward through the scorecards. As the title of this section asks: who connects each HOQ? The people working behind the scenes make it happen, and they are representing different business functions as we traverse through the different HOQs. Figure 11.5 illustrates the representation of each distinct function being involved across each HOQ.

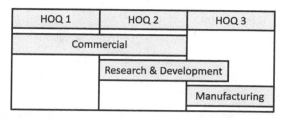

FIGURE 11.5
Primary business functions involved building and defining each HOQ.

It is important to note that the overlapping of functions becomes a hand-off of knowledge and information between those two business groups. For example, HOQ1 is driven primarily by the commercial business function comprised of sales and marketing. HOQ2 will need input from HOQ1. HOQ2 will combine research and development (R&D) information with data from HOQ1 gathered by sales and marketing. This overlap creates the conversation between the two business functions: commercial and R&D. A similar overlap occurs in HOQ3 with R&D and manufacturing.

This connectivity doesn't end in HOQ3, the Manufacturing house. The last house has methods to connect the customer to the factory floor. Let's share a few examples on how we can connect the factory to the customer. I was recently trying on jeans at a store and noticed a piece of paper in my pocket. I pulled out of the small paper, and it said, "QC PASS 62." Being the quality conscious person that I am, I was impressed. I looked at the paper and nodding in agreement with inspector 62. That connected me with the company and decided to purchase the pair of jeans. These types of surprises occur more often than you think.

Here are more examples. We spend one-third of our life on mattresses, and the people that make them know that. They want to proudly display their workmanship on it, and the one I bought has a cloth label draped prominently on the front edge. It reads: **Handcrafted in Indiana Master Craftsman Felicie Gregory**. A paper bag looks simple and disposable. That may not be the case when the bottom of the bag not only shows proudly the brand of the bag but also the person that made it. Another place I encountered unexpectedly the voice of the factory floor was on a box of tea. This box of tea bags not only contains exceptional quality tea but also the company wants to connect with you, the consumer. They did it in the following manner: **tea packed by: Juliana W, Best enjoyed by: February 2019**. Figure 11.6a–c shows the pictures of the proud employee showcasing their products.

(a)

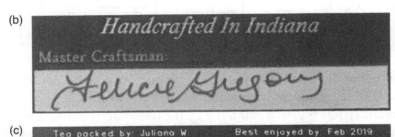

FIGURE 11.6
(a) QC PASS 62. (b) Handcrafted in Indiana. (c) Tea packed by: Juliana W.

I, as a customer of all four examples, became connected to the factory floor with those statements. The deliberately chosen words made a connection between me as the customer and them as the people on the factory floor. Let's dig deeper by studying the words used on those statements. The mattress label has the term, handcrafted in Indiana; it brings a sense of a person using their time and effort to make the mattress for me. Emphasizing that the workmanship is in Indiana not only informs us that was built in the United States of America but also tells us specifically a location in the Midwest. Master Craftsman Felicie Gregory puts in perspective that a master craftsman did my mattress. If that wasn't enough, Felicie Gregory's signature is at the bottom of the label, giving a sense of pride of the workmanship directed at me, the end user. Analyzing the tea box descriptions shares a similar structure. We have the person that handled the box described as tea packed by Juliana W, putting a name to the contents of what is in the box. To make it even more personal, Juliana wants you to enjoy the tea by a February 2019. Instead of using best buy a specific date to show its level of freshness, they used the key word enjoy, making the use of the tea a personable and enjoyable moment.

It's a firm reminder that people make products and they shared with me that human touch. What can you do to connect your product or your employees to your customers?

11.3.2 Training

Training brings your employees and customers to a common level of understanding. We are dealing with many metrics placed in several HOQs. Establishing a common definition is important; training is the mechanism used to create those descriptions. If we do not have a formal and periodic training, we may drift slowly away from the original intent of the metric. To prevent this elusive drift of what the metric means, we must first define what the metrics are. An operational definition must exist for each one and its method of measurement. The SOP documents the process on how to measure.

Figure 11.5 shows how the different business functions are involved with different HOQs. These business functions can own the documentation for the metrics and methods used in that HOQ. Since the functions own the metrics and documentation on how to do it correctly, they can also own and deliver the training, aligning the business functions with the metrics and its related SOPs. For example, if the focus is about HOQ3, the Manufacturing house, each Process Variable (PV) metric is described and analyzed. The training is delivered by the manufacturing personnel.

Although we speak about the metrics aligned on a specific HOQ, we must not lose sight of the broader picture. These metrics are dependent from other metrics that came from a previous HOQ. In other words, as the manufacturing experts train about the PVs in HOQ3; these also show in the main room of HOQ3 the association of the PV metrics with the QC metrics, as shown in Figure 11.7. Recall that the QC metrics came from HOQ2. The HOQ has interdependencies from the other house reiterating their shared interactions among all those HOQs.

Remember this training may have an internal focus to enhance the knowledge of your employees in that department or function. Those functions that have direct or indirect contact with the customer can benefit by training their customers on that HOQ and selected metrics, especially those variables that are significant to your customer.

A last note, to complement the training, emphasize the different variations of HOQs. We've seen earlier in this book the three standard HOQs. This chapter presented the HOQ flow down. Later in Chapter 12, we will describe variations of several types of HOQs. Remember training keeps us proactively on track to deliver results expected from our customer. We learned many angles of what freedom within a framework means. We also

House of Quality 3
Manufacturing House

Quality Control Metric	Weight / Priority	Manually added RMs	Automatically added RMs	Reactor Temperature	Reaction time in reactor	Reactor agitator speed	Cooldown tank temperature	Cooldown tank agitator speed	Complete order and shipped on time
Metric improvement direction or target →		•	•	•	•	•	▼	•	▲
Process Variables Target and Unit of Measure →		Target Amount and Type (lb)	Target Amount and Type (lb)	255-285 (°F)	110 - 130 (min)	45 (RPM)	Cool to below 80 (°F)	85 (RPM)	>95%
Gel Time @ 250 F	25.3%	9	9	9	6	3	3	3	9
Number of Cracks	19.4%	9	9	9	9	9	6	6	9
Viscosity	16.5%	9	9	9	9	6	9	9	9
Orange Peel Appearance	16.1%	6	9	6	6	6	3	3	9
60-Degree Gloss	22.6%	6	6	9	6	3			9
CALCULATED IMPORTANCE →		7.84	8.32	8.52	7.08	5.14	3.89	3.89	9
Rank →		4	3	2	5	6	7	8	1

FIGURE 11.7
HOQ3 relates PV metrics with QC metrics.

have created a clear line of sight from the customer to the factory floor and the factory floor back to the customer. To sustain these gains, we must invest time to train our employees and customers. The next chapter provides variations of the HOQs.

12

The Complexity of the Product and HOQs

We now look at the variations of the number of Houses of Quality (HOQs) based on the developed product. Complexity will be a key factor in determining the type and number of houses needed. We have been only using three HOQs throughout this book. In this chapter, we will discover the rationale to evaluate whether to use one, three, or four HOQs. Two houses are not normally used, so we will not spend time on that topic. The number of HOQs will be dependent on the complexity of the product being developed. Normally, a less complex product will use a single HOQ, while a moderately complex product typically requires three HOQs, and finally, a complex product uses four HOQs.

Additionally, the HOQ will grow with added rooms to help evaluate your product in more detail. This evaluation not only analyzes your product attributes against your customer's needs, as we did in an earlier chapter, but also rates the item against your competitors, defining exactly which attribute needs attention to maintain your competitive edge.

12.1 LESS COMPLEX PRODUCT

Products that don't have much complexity can also take advantage of the HOQ structure and information. To visualize this approach, we will use the example of a somewhat simple product such as Post-it notes. These are square pads of paper that measure about 2 by 2 in. (76 by 76 mm). Each Post-it has a self-adhesive edge that can affix to many smooth surfaces and peeled off easily and also it can be reapplied to another location. The paper used is equivalent to a basic copy paper with a weight between 18 and 20 lb

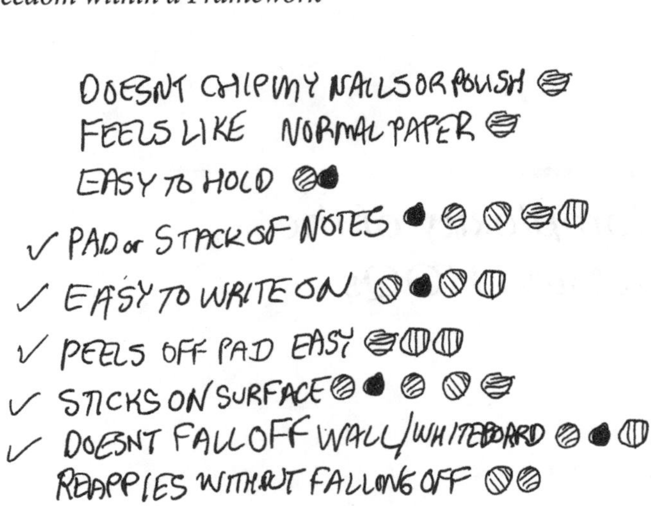

DOESNT CHIP MY NAILS OR POLISH ☞
FEELS LIKE NORMAL PAPER ☞
EASY TO HOLD ●●
✓ PAD or STACK OF NOTES ● ● ● ●●
✓ EASY TO WRITE ON ● ●● ●
✓ PEELS OFF PAD EASY ☞●●
✓ STICKS ON SURFACE ●● ● ● ●
✓ DOESNT FALL OFF WALL/WHITEBOARD ● ● ●
REAPPLIES WITHOUT FALLING OFF ●●

FIGURE 12.1
Post-it VOC list and multivotes.

and can be of diverse colors. Before going any further, we must understand what the customer expects from the product and how they use it.

After listening to the customer from surveys and focus groups, we were able to know their requirements for the Post-it notes. Figure 12.1 captures the Voice of the Customer (VOC) list and multivoting, and the most important ones are highlighted. The steps for the exercise apply the concepts detailed in Chapter 2. After reviewing the count of votes, the team decided that the top five will become the key VOCs for this product (indicated with the check mark on the left of the VOC list in Figure 12.1).

Now that we have a clear understanding of customer's requirements of the product, we can now focus on the technical details of the Post-it note. The sticky edge, considered the most innovated component of this product, needs more specifics to define how much force is needed to properly pull the Post-it off the surface. Figure 12.2 shows more specifics about the location of the adhesive strip and the stacking of the papers on the pad. The observation of the people in the focus group helped us identify several behaviors and how the Post-it is applied to the working surface, typically people wrote first on the paper before applying it to the surface. Therefore, we need to make the pad comfortable to hold and stiff enough, so the person can write on the pad while holding. Table 12.1 and Figures 12.1 show details and specifications of this simpler product.

The Post-it should have enough tack to hold its weight if it is adhered to a vertical surface, and simultaneously, it should be easy to peel off. Two predominant patterns emerged on how people peeled off the Post-it. One method is

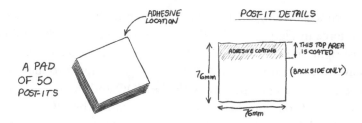

FIGURE 12.2
Post-it adhesive details.

TABLE 12.1

Post-it VOC List and Multivote

VOC Concept	Number of Votes	Voted Top 5
Many colors	0	No
Doesn't chip my nails or polish	1	No
Feels like normal paper	1	No
Easy to hold	2	No
Pad or stack of notes	5	Yes
Easy to write on	4	Yes
Peels off the pad easy	3	Yes
Sticks on surface	5	Yes
Doesn't fall off wall/whiteboard	3	Yes
Reapplies without falling off	2	No

pulling straight up by holding the center of the paper, and the other is pulling it curl up by holding it on one corner of the paper pad. Figure 12.3 depicts the Post-it removal methods. Each action has a specific amount of force needed to pull the paper. Pulling the Post-it straight up requires between 90 and 94 g of force. The curl up method uses 20–25 g of force, requiring significantly less amount of force to peel off when compared to pull up. These ranges are the optimal values. We shared in the focus group five distinct levels of tackiness, and the ranges shown in the figure happen to be the second from the bottom. The top three had too much strength causing sometimes to rip the paper. The

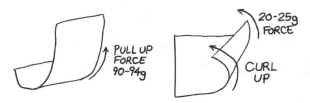

FIGURE 12.3
Post-it pull force details.

ripping occurs depending on the angle used to pull the Post-it. The indicated values of force in Figure 12.3 hit the sweet spot, not too sticky and not too loose, just right, so the Post-it will not fall off the wall (Table 12.2).

We have now a full picture of this somewhat simple product. We captured the customer's perspective with the VOC and the technical details by working with our product development team. The HOQ flow down combines the VOC and Critical to Quality (CTQ) metrics as shown in Figure 12.4. This process is comparable to the methods described in Chapter 11 for the HOQ flow down.

As seen in the flow down, some of the attributes satisfy multiple VOCs, and multiple CTQs can help a single VOC. Some of the listed VOCs have been addressed although these receive little to no votes. Color is one those attributes that received no votes, and it is a feature offered with the product. Next to each CTQ displays the range of values needed to balance all the properties of the product. This equilibrium of attributes will address the top five VOCs captured through the multivoting, and hopefully, it will meet or exceed customer satisfaction.

TABLE 12.2

List of Attributes and Values that Define a Post-it

Attributes	Values
Post-it size	76 by 76 mm
Post-it adhesive area	15 mm high by width of paper (one side only)
Curl up pull force	20–25 g of force
Pull up pull force	90–94 g of force
Paper weight	18–20 lb paper
Color	Varies

House of Quality flow down

Customer House HOQ1		
What does the customer say they want?	Critical to Quality for the customer's needs (how does the customer determine satisfaction?)	
Voice of Customer	**Critical to Quality**	Values
Pad or stack of notes	Post-it size	76 mm by 76 mm
Easy to write on	Post-it adhesive area	15 mm high by width of paper (one side only)
Peels off the pad easy	Curl up pull force	20 – 25 g of force
Sticks on surface	Pull up pull force	90 – 94 g of force
Doesn't fall off wall / whiteboard	Paper weight	18 – 20 lb paper
	Color	Varies

FIGURE 12.4
Post-it HOQ flow down.

12.1.1 One House of Quality

Elements of the HOQ have been created with the flow down as shown in Figure 12.4. We now rearrange the VOC and the CTQ following the structure shared in Chapter 5. Figure 12.5a illustrates the completed HOQ.

We also have the CTQ ranked values created from the scores given by the relationships between CTQs and VOCs, entered in the main room of the HOQ as demonstrated in Figure 12.5b.

(a)

House of Quality 1
Customer House

	Metric improvement direction or target →		Post-it size	Post-it adhesive area	Curl up pull force	Pull up pull force	Paper weight	Color	
			•	•	▼	▼	•	•	
	Critical to Quality Metric, Target and Unit of Measure →		76 mm by 76 mm	15 mm high by width of paper (one side only)	20 – 25 g of force	90 – 94 g of force	18 – 20 lb paper	Varies	
	Voice of Customer Wants/ Needs	Weight / Priority							
171	Pad or stack of notes	9	9	1	3	3	3		
63	Easy to write on	3	3				9	9	
99	Peels off the pad easy	3	3	9	9	9	3		
279	Sticks on surface	9	1	9	9	9	3		
117	Doesn't fall off wall / whiteboard	3	3	9	9	9	9		
			117	144	162	162	117	27	
			4	3	1	2	5	6	

(b)

CTQ Rank	Critical to Quality Metrics (HOWS)	Relative Weight
1	Curl up pull force	22.2%
2	Pull up pull force	22.2%
3	Post-it adhesive area	19.8%
4	Post-it size	16.0%
5	Paper weight	16.0%
6	Color	3.7%

FIGURE 12.5
(a) One HOQ for Post-it. (b) CTQ rankings Pareto chart for HOQ1.

Since this product is not complicated, only one HOQ and the flow down is enough to create a relationship between the product's characteristics and the customer's needs.

12.2 MODERATELY COMPLEX PRODUCT

Throughout the book, we explored in detail the brightly colored plastic tubes made by our fictitious customer, Tubing Experts. Our company, Liquid Paint Specialists, another hypothetical business, makes the paint that is applied on the plastic tube to provide the finished color and appearance that our customer will desire. This coating or paint would fall under the moderately complex product. How did we determine that the coating is moderately complex? It depends on the product that you manufacture and how it will be applied by the customer or end user. One way to look at this arrangement is, if your product can serve many customers or platforms; we call that one to many. The reverse is also true for a moderately complex product. Many products can provide several features for the same customer application or need, in other words, many to one. Let me illustrate both with coating examples.

12.2.1 One to Many

In the coating industry, several technologies exist to marry the needs of the product substrate and the final topcoat visible to the end user. To highlight the one to many relationships, we will use the coating technology of polyurethane resin (PUR). PUR, as it is typically abbreviated, is a well-established product that can help protect the wood substrate in its many forms. It can protect wood interiors such as floors and kitchen cabinets. Also, it has applications that protect wood exposed to the elements, like garage doors, decks, and windows. PUR can even be applied to guard against harsh marine environments and protect boats and other equivalent applications.

12.2.2 Many to One

Since we used the example of wood before, let's expand that concept to highlight the many to one association. We can use many coating technologies to affect a single type of wood application such as kitchen cabinets. The types of coating technologies used on cabinetry are numerous. Two major groups are water-based paints or coatings, and the second are oil- or solvent-based coatings. Under these two headings, many technologies exist depending on the desired look, application method, durability, and any other property for the kitchen cabinet. The aforementioned polyurethane falls under the solvent-based coating and provides a tough surface layer with an amber tone enhancing the wood grain. Other oil-based paints are epoxies, providing a very hard, glossy, and durable finish, covering the natural wood grain (opaque formulation) tinted to your custom color. Just to name a few, other solvent-based colors are alkyd-based paints, silicone epoxy, etc. Another consideration when choosing a solvent-borne coating are the evaporating vapors which can be harmful, and ventilation will be needed. Because of those volatile compounds, the water-based paints have a much lower range of fumes. These coatings are also known as latex paint, and to name a couple under this category are acrylic paint and alkyd enamels. This expanded example provided you a good understanding on how the many coating technologies can help solve the need for one type of application.

12.2.3 Three Houses of Quality

A moderately complex product are products that don't have a clear line of sight of the needs of the customer. Product development and manufacturing needs to coordinate inputs from various business functions. It was the premise of this book to know how to thread the VOC to the factory floor. We developed ways to distill from many business functional groups their information and summarized those in the HOQs. As a refresher, Figure 12.6 shows the three HOQs, and Figure 12.7 has the HOQ flow down.

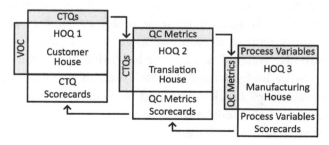

FIGURE 12.6
Three HOQs connected with scorecard flow up.

House of Quality flow down			
Customer House HOQ1		Translation House, HOQ2	Manufacturing House, HOQ3
What does the customer say they want?	Critical to Quality for the customer's needs (how does the customer determine satisfaction?)	How will we make sure we meet the customers' requirements (CTQs)? (what must the product do to meet the CTQs?)	How will we **control the** manufacturing **process** to ensure we meet the QC metrics?
Voice of Customer	Critical to Quality	Quality Control Metric	Process Variables
Product is within specs Our product improves your productivity Mileage made today Even coating thickness Appearance	Crack rates Cure time Tube integrity Plugged spray nozzles Plugged filters Sticky tubes Consistency of cured film build Holiday testing	Gel Time @ 250 F Number of Cracks Viscosity Orange Peel Appearance 60-Degree Gloss	Complete order and shipped on time Reactor Temperature Automatically added RMs Manually added RMs Reaction time in reactor Reactor agitator speed Cooldown tank temperature Cooldown tank agitator speed

FIGURE 12.7
HOQ flow down.

12.3 COMPLEX PRODUCT

Complex products, in the broader sense of the term, can be viewed as a combination of multiple components grouped together to make a whole. Each part can be simple products or moderately complex. A refrigerator is an example of a complex product. It has multiple parts that all fit together and work in harmony to function properly. For instance, the electrical system, comprised of the motor and compressor, needs to work in coordination with the freezer section of the refrigerator, providing the desired temperature. In this section of the chapter, we will expand on these complex examples and show methods on how to use the HOQ in a more extended manner.

12.3.1 Complex Products Subsystems

A complex product is primarily a combination of subsystems assembled together. Our body is a fitting example of a very complex system. We have many subsystems, and each one has a specific task. For example, the cardiovascular system has a beating heart that moves the vital blood around our entire body to maintain life on all the cells it touches. The digestive system helps break down food to its chemical components to provide nutrients to the body's cells to promote energy, growth, and healing. These two, combined with the many other systems our body has, work in harmony creating a network of interdependent relationships to keep us healthy and alive. Because of the complexity of each of the human being's subsystem, the field of medicine has specialized on each one of these areas to clearly understand those subsections. We will use this same thinking, applying the expertise and understanding to connect the subsystems with the whole.

A more complex item is a transportation product such as an automobile. A car has many subsystems: engine, transmission, passenger safety, wheels and suspension, electrical and wiring, audio and navigation systems to name a few. Figure 12.8 shows how these collections of subsystems interact to have a holistic view of the car. The transmission will need to capture the input from the engine HOQs, making the connectivity fluid across the series of HOQs.

The subsystems use the HOQs to analyze the product from VOC to manufacturing conditions as described before in this book. Some customers have a strong opinion about the engine specifications. The engine HOQs translate the VOC regarding performance metrics, flowing that information from house to house, so that it can be built in a competitive and cost-effective manner. Now the other system, the transmission, will need to capture some inputs from the engine HOQs, making the connectivity fluid across the two sets of HOQs. These two subsystems are now interconnected.

Continuing with another subsystem, passenger safety has VOCs from several perspectives. The VOC can come from different perspectives. In the United States, one voice is from industry regulators that test the vehicle to ensure they meet certain thresholds of safety. They ensure that the "cage of safety" is maintained intact by submitting the car to several crash tests with crash test dummies to collect critical information. The "cage of safety" is also known in the racing community as the roll cage.

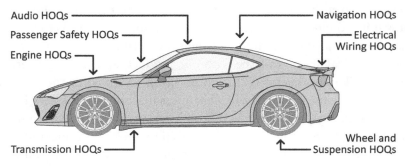

FIGURE 12.8
Car subsystems and HOQs.

A roll cage's purpose is to protect the driver and passengers from vehicle rupture in case of a roll over or side impact. This data, combined with the drivers' and passengers' input, creates a very thorough input into HOQ1, helping define better CTQ metrics. Electrical and wiring will look at all the customer's needs for illumination, door locks, sensors to name a few. HOQ1 captures these VOCs and threaded to the last HOQ. The same thought process can be applied to the other subsystems of wheels, suspension, audio, and navigation.

Compiling all the HOQs will provide the producer of the product a multifaceted view of their product with tremendous details. The details will allow the maker of these items know their customers further by creating very customized surveys to get inputs on a very specific topic. The inputs can help spur future innovation and customer satisfaction. Product breakthroughs can be discovered by using the techniques discussed in Chapter 2, the Kano model. The Delighters are key in bringing something to the customer that they didn't anticipate. You get to know more of the needs of your customers and foresee a potential need before they can articulate it.

Although we looked each subsystem in detail from end to end from the VOC to manufacturing, we shouldn't be looking at each in isolation. These need to be combined to ensure that the product fits all the components to make it whole. It is like the human body example given earlier. The circulatory system needs to be in harmony with the digestive system and the nervous system and the immune system, etc. Missing a subsystem will be detrimental to the success of the body functioning properly. If a small part of our body is not functioning well, it will be exhibited as a slight discomfort or a blemish, a harmless or annoying situation. On the other hand, the slight uneasiness may be the beginning of a more serious ailment. A health professional helps validate the person's condition to know if it is dangerous or benign. This same approach needs to be taken when looking at these complex systems. Sometimes, our customer will become critical about an issue with our product, and we may overreact to solve it like it was serious "life-threatening" event while the customer expressed only the equivalent of a harmless discomfort. It is very important to put in perspective the VOC and listen well. Let me leave you with a quote from Stephen R. Covey, "You listen for feeling, for meaning. You listen for behavior. You use your right brain as well as your left. You sense, you intuit, you feel."

12.3.2 VOCs and CTQs with Competitor Information

In this book, we have highlighted the relationship of a product with the customer, and the product with many different business functions that helps make the item all the way to the factory floor. In the real world, we have competitors who want our customers to buy their products. The competition may offer certain features in their product that may be beneficial to the customer, and because of that, we may lose the competitive edge we once had.

HOQ1 has a treasure trove of great data that can be used to understand how our product compares to our competitor's. Let's start with the VOC by reverting to our company, Liquid Paint Specialists, which makes coatings for our customer Tubing Experts. We built HOQ1 to capture the VOC, and we were able to learn which CTQs drive the needs for that product. The main room of HOQ1 describes this relationship. These details are the quantitative impact of our product on the VOC and CTQs and how each other relate. Now, all that data can be used to learn the specifics about our competition. To extract that information, let's have our own customer inform us about their likes and dislikes about the product they use and how it compares with our competitors. Of course, this depends on how good of a relationship you have with your customer. We will make the assumption that the relationship is friendly, and the information flow is open and fluid. They answer in a scale of 0–5 on how our product performs in their process. The scale 0–5 in Table 12.3 shows the context of what each numerical value refers to.

These values are entered to the right of the main room of the HOQ as shown in Figure 12.9. This room, referred affectionately as the back porch, contains the summary of our customer's input of our competitors.

Next, we need to compare our product to each customer, referred as the VOC gap. Figure 12.10 shows the VOC gap as the last column to the right.

TABLE 12.3

Evaluation of Competitors Numerical Scale

Numerical Scale	Evaluation of Competitors
5	Best in class
4	Very good
3	Average
2	Mediocre
1	Poor
0	Unusable

House of Quality 1
Customer House

Metric improvement direction or target →		▼	●	▲	▲	▼	●	●	▼				
Critical to Quality Metric, Target and Unit of Measure →		1 crack per 1000ft	120 seconds or less	Minimum 90%	Red = partly clogged, Yellow = min clogging, Green = clean	0 to 2 psi (>2 change)	Yes or No	1.0 mil +/- 0.3 mil	0% and 1%				
Voice of Customer Wants/ Needs	Weight / Priority	Crack rates	Cure time	Tube integrity	Plugged spray nozzles	Plugged filters	Sticky tubes	Consistency of cured film build	Holiday testing	Our Company	Competitor 1	Competitor 2	Competitor 3
28 Product is within specs.	1	9		6			1	6	6	4	4	3	4
405 Our product improves your productivity.	9		9	9	3		9	6	9	4	3	5	3
522 Mileage made today.	9	3	9	9	9	1	9	9	9	4	3	5	3
108 Even coating thickness.	3			9	9			9	9	5	4	5	3
33 Appearance.	3			3	3	1		3	1	3	3	4	3
CALCULATED IMPORTANCE →		36	162	204	144	13	162	177	198				
Rank →		7	4	1	6	8	5	3	2				

FIGURE 12.9
HOQ1 with VOCs of competitors.

House of Quality 1
Customer House

Metric improvement direction or target →		▼	●	▲	▲	▼	●	●	▼					
Critical to Quality Metric, Target and Unit of Measure →		1 crack per 1000ft	120 seconds or less	Minimum 90%	Red = partly clogged, Yellow = min clogging, Green = clean	0 to 2 psi (>2 change)	Yes or No	1.0 mil +/- 0.3 mil	0% and 1%					
Voice of Customer Wants/ Needs	Weight / Priority	Crack rates	Cure time	Tube integrity	Plugged spray nozzles	Plugged filters	Sticky tubes	Consistency of cured film build	Holiday testing	Our Company	Competitor 1	Competitor 2	Competitor 3	VOC Gap
28 Product is within specs.	1	9		6			1	6	6	4	4	3	4	0
405 Our product improves your productivity.	9		9	9	3		9	6	9	4	3	5	3	-1
522 Mileage made today.	9	3	9	9	9	1	9	9	9	4	3	5	3	-1
108 Even coating thickness.	3			9	9			9	9	5	4	5	3	0
33 Appearance.	3			3	3	1		3	1	3	3	4	3	-1
CALCULATED IMPORTANCE →		36	162	204	144	13	162	177	198					
Rank →		7	4	1	6	8	5	3	2					

FIGURE 12.10
HOQ1 with VOCs of competitors and VOC gap.

This gap indicates if our product attribute for that specific VOC is positive, meaning that we are doing better than the best competitor, or negative if we are doing worse than the competition. A third option would be zero indicating we are matching that VOC request with the highest value of all competitors. To understand how to calculate the VOC gap, Figure 12.11 shows these steps.

Let us now learn about the CTQ gap. Interpreting and evaluating the CTQ gap is like the VOC gap. The CTQ competitive information can be derived from our customer or collected from within our company. Most likely these values are compiled from within our company. The members in our commercial function will have a good understanding of the CTQs. They attend typically trade shows and conferences to enrich our product portfolio and identify potential gaps. These gaps can be CTQ related or can be of an entire product offering. Another internal group that will be able to help evaluate the competition's CTQs is the research and development (R&D) function. Our R&D team members often have product performance test to quantify if our product is competitive in the marketplace.

As calculated earlier for the VOC gap, using our company as the reference point, ask if the competitors are better, worse or that same as us? Figure 12.12 shows the steps and calculations on how we arrive to the CTQ gap for each line item. We now have the basement of the house completed with all the competition CTQ information. The complete view of our competitors' benchmark is shown in Figure 12.13.

Voice of Customer Wants/ Needs	Weight / Priority	Crack rates	Cure time	Tube integrity	Plugged spray nozzles	Plugged filters	Sticky tubes	Consistency of cured film build	Holiday testing		Our Company	Competitor 1	Competitor 2	Competitor 3		VOC Gap
Product is within specs.	1	9			6		1		6	6							0
Our product improves your productivity.	9		9	9	3			9	6	9							-1
Mileage made today.	9	3	9	9	9	1	9	9	9		4	3	5	3		-1	⬅
Even coating thickness.	3			9	9			9	9							0
Appearance.	3			3	3	1		3	1							-1

VOC gap = Our Score - Maximum (Competitor's Score)

VOC gap = 4 - Maximum (3, 5, 3)

VOC gap = 4 - 5

VOC gap = -1

FIGURE 12.11
How to calculate the VOC gap in HOQ1.

Voice of Customer Wants/ Needs	Weight / Priority	Crack rates	Cure time	Tube integrity	Plugged spray nozzles	Plugged filters	Sticky tubes	Consistency of cured film build	Holiday testing	
28 Product is within specs.	1	9		6		1		6	6	
405 Our product improves your productivity.	9		9	9	3		9	6	9	
522 Mileage made today.	9	3	9	9	9	1	9	9	9	
108 Even coating thickness.	3			9	9			9	9	
33 Appearance.	3			3	3	1		3	1	
CALCULATED IMPORTANCE →		36	162	204	144	13	162	177	198	
Rank →		7	4	1	6	8	5	3	2	
Our Company		4	5	4	4	5	5	**5**	4	
Competitor 1		3	4	2	4	4	1	**1**	2	
Competitor 2		5	5	5	5	5	5	**3**	3	
Competitor 3		4	5	4	4	5	5	**4**	4	
CTQ Gap		-1	0	-1	-1	0	0	**1**	0	

$CTQ\ gap = Our\ Score - Maximum\ (Competitor's\ Score)$

$CTQ\ gap = 5 - Maximum\ (1, 3, 4)$

$CTQ\ gap = 5 - 4$

$CTQ\ gap = 1$

FIGURE 12.12
How to calculate the CTQ gap in HOQ1.

House of Quality 1
Customer House

Metric improvement direction or target →	▼	●	▲	▲	▼	●	●	▼					
Critical to Quality Metric, Target and Unit of Measure →	1 crack per 1000ft	120 seconds or less	Minimum 90%	Red = partly clogged, Yellow = min clogging, Green = clean	0 to 2 psi (>2 change)	Yes or No	1.0 mil +/- 0.3 mil	0% and 1%					

Voice of Customer Wants/ Needs	Weight / Priority	Crack rates	Cure time	Tube integrity	Plugged spray nozzles	Plugged filters	Sticky tubes	Consistency of cured film build	Holiday testing	Our Company	Competitor 1	Competitor 2	Competitor 3	VOC Gap
28 Product is within specs.	1	9		6		1		6	6	4	4	3	4	0
405 Our product improves your productivity.	9		9	9	3		9	6	9	4	3	5	3	-1
522 Mileage made today.		3	9	9	9	1	9	9	9	4	3	5	3	-1
108 Even coating thickness.	3			9	9			9	9	5	4	5	3	0
33 Appearance.	3			3	3	1		3	1	3	3	4	3	-1
CALCULATED IMPORTANCE →		36	162	204	144	13	162	177	198					
Rank →		7	4	1	6	8	5	3	2					
Our Company		4	5	4	4	5	5	5	4					
Competitor 1		3	4	2	4	4	1	1	2					
Competitor 2		5	5	5	5	5	5	3	3					
Competitor 3		4	5	4	4	5	5	4	4					
CTQ Gap		-1	0	-1	-1	0	0	1	0					

FIGURE 12.13
HOQ1 with VOCs and CTQs of competitors.

Having the competitive information by each CTQ and each VOC keeps us informed of our relative position in the market. This type of analysis can expand to the other HOQs to gain insights in other areas such as manufacturing, research, and supply chain. Benchmarking, trade shows, and industry research news help gather the knowledge of that industry. Finally, if you are not doing this type of in-depth competitive analysis, you may risk that your product becomes obsolete and displaced by a competitor.

12.3.3 HOQ1 with a Roof

We have just added more rooms to our original HOQ1. We started with the main room in order to relate the VOC with the CTQ metrics. This main room gave a clear line of sight about the relationship between the two metrics. Also, it gave us a priority and ranking of each one of those two metrics based on its level of impact. That relationship remained mainly between the customer and us as the supplier. As said before, in the real world, we have competitors and that necessitates us to expand the house with more rooms. We added the back porch to know more about the VOC, from our customer's perspective, and how our product performs against our competition. Later another room was added, the basement, to know how our CTQs compare to our competitors.

It is ironic that we speak about a HOQ, or specifically about a house with many rooms and we haven't added a roof to protect all the contents in the home. Well, the time has come to add a roof to our house. The roof will capture the interactions among the CTQs. You may ask, what good is that? Are we just adding another relationship matrix so we can have a roof and call it officially a house? Not quite. The roof will become the most important part of the house just like a real house keeping the elements away from penetrating into our rooms.

The CTQs have properties that were explored comprehensively earlier in Chapter 4. Each one of these properties can interfere with one another and either diminish or enhance those characteristics. Figure 12.14 shows how we can learn about those combinations by structuring the roof above the CTQs.

We will take a CTQ attribute and observe how it affects another CTQ. Based on that relationship, it can have a positive or negative impact. Finally, it could have no interaction at all which would indicate that those two CTQs are completely independent of each other. Table 12.4 captures all five options, four levels of interactions, or no interaction at all.

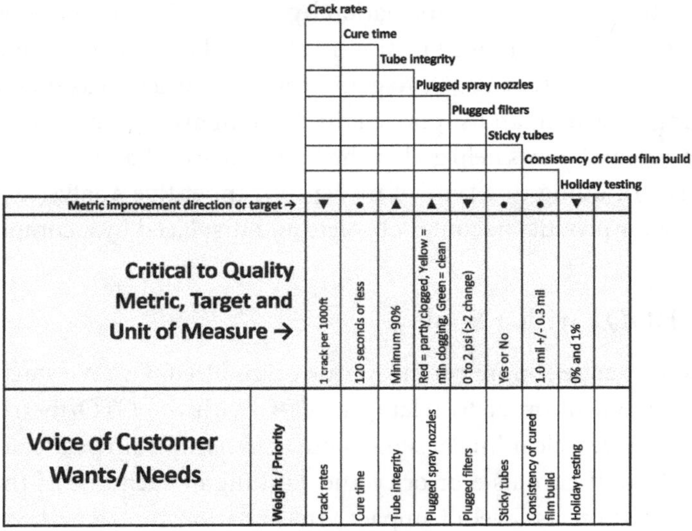

FIGURE 12.14
The roof of HOQ1.

	Crack rates	Cure time	Tube integrity	Plugged spray nozzles	Plugged filters	Sticky tubes	Consistency of cured film build	Holiday testing
Metric improvement direction or target →	▼	•	▲	▲	▼	•	•	▼

Critical to Quality Metric, Target and Unit of Measure →	1 crack per 1000ft	120 seconds or less	Minimum 90%	Red = partly clogged, Yellow = min clogging, Green = clean	0 to 2 psi (>2 change)	Yes or No	1.0 mil +/- 0.3 mil	0% and 1%
Voice of Customer Wants/Needs — Weight / Priority	Crack rates	Cure time	Tube integrity	Plugged spray nozzles	Plugged filters	Sticky tubes	Consistency of cured film build	Holiday testing

TABLE 12.4

Metrics Interactions on the Roof

Symbol Scale	Evaluation of Competitors
+ +	Strong positive
+	Positive
−	Negative
− −	Strong negative
Empty	No interaction

The evaluation of the pair of CTQs on the roof is done by asking two questions.

Question 1: Is there an impact of CTQ A affecting CTQ B? If this question is yes, then answer question 2. If there is no relationship, do not score it; keep it empty.

Question 2: If CTQ A goes up, how does it affect CTQ B (does it go up or down)? If it is up, it affects CTQ B positively. If it goes down, it affects CTQ B negatively. Lastly, we clarify the strength of the relationship by asking a follow-up question: how much of a change is it, slightly or strongly?

An example will help understand these relationships. The Voice of our Customer mentioned that **Sticky tubes** (a term that the customer calls tubes that are not totally cured and are still tacky to the touch) was a key attribute that caused issues. To address this problem, the roof of HOQ1 relates **Sticky tubes** with **Cure time**. Referring to the left image of Figure 12.15 shows how to read and interpret the CTQs on the roof by applying the two structured questions. Is there an impact of **Cure Time** affecting **Sticky Tubes**? Yes, cure time has a direct impact to sticky tubes. The second question: if **Cure Time** goes up, how does it affect **Sticky Tubes**? The answer is: when **Cure time** goes up, **Sticky tubes** are less tacky. These two CTQs are inversely proportional. By rephrasing the interaction, the opposite way, less cure time increases the amount of sticky tubes. We then clarify the degree of the relationship. How much of a change? This CTQ interaction has a strong negative relationship, shown with the double minus symbol (– –).

The second example shown in the right image of Figure 12.15 is a strong positive impact. The example used here came from the discussions shown earlier in Chapter 4. The **Plugged spray nozzles** can create holidays. Holidays are defined as pinholes and voids on a painted thin-film coating. Following the same two-question approach. Is there an impact of **Plugged spray nozzles** affecting **Holiday testing**? Yes, plugged spray nozzles has a direct impact to holiday testing. The second question: If **Plugged spray nozzles** goes up, how does it affect **Holiday testing**? If plugged spray nozzles goes up, **Holiday testing** also increases, which is viewed as a positive relationship. We then explain how strong that relationship is, and it is a strong positive relationship shown with the two positive signs (+ +). In Figure 12.16, you will find the HOQ with the roof completed with the competitor information.

Now we have a complete house with a roof, putting in perspective which CTQs can improve another shown with a + or strongly improves another shown as (+ +). Additionally, when using the basement information of our competitors, we can see if those strongly positives or strongly negatives are affecting our competitive stance in the market. Right away we can see if we have leadership positions or not, keeping competitors in our sights and hopefully away.

The double minus symbol (– –) was made from two CTQs not cooperating with each other; to put it in another way, these strongly negative combinations are having the most destructive influence on our product. It is because of that negative impact; we will turn to the next section and learn from that relationship, in other words, making lemonade from lemons.

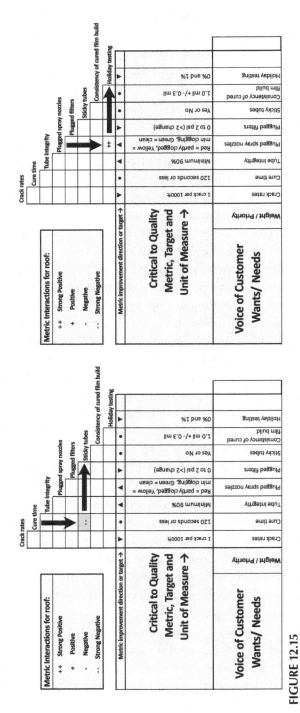

FIGURE 12.15

CTQ interactions on the roof of HOQI.

House of Quality 1
Customer House

Metric Interactions for roof:	
++	Strong Positive
+	Positive
-	Negative
--	Strong Negative

Crack rates
+ Cure time
++ Tube integrity
+ Plugged spray nozzles
+ - ++ Plugged filters
+ -- - + Sticky tubes
+ + + -- + Consistency of cured film build
+ - ++ + + -- Holiday testing

Metric improvement direction or target → ▼ ● ▲ ▲ ▼ ● ● ▼

Critical to Quality Metric, Target and Unit of Measure →

Voice of Customer Wants/ Needs	Weight / Priority	Crack rates	Cure time	Tube integrity	Plugged spray nozzles	Plugged filters	Sticky tubes	Consistency of cured film build	Holiday testing	Our Company	Competitor 1	Competitor 2	Competitor 3	VOC Gap
		1 crack per 1000ft	120 seconds or less	Minimum 90%	Red = partly clogged, Yellow = min clogging, Green = clean	0 to 2 psi (>2 change)	Yes or No	1.0 mil +/- 0.3 mil	0% and 1%					
28 Product is within specs.	1	9		6		1		6	6	4	4	3	4	0
405 Our product improves your productivity.	9		9	9	3		9	6	9	4	3	5	3	-1
522 Mileage made today.	9	3	9	9	9	1	9	9	9	4	3	5	3	-1
108 Even coating thickness.	3			9	9			9	9	5	4	3	3	0
33 Appearance.	3			3	3	1		3	1	3	3	4	3	-1
CALCULATED IMPORTANCE →		36	162	204	144	13	162	177	198					
Rank →		7	4	1	6	8	5	3	2					
Our Company		4	5	4	4	5	5	5	4					
Competitor 1		3	4	2	4	4	1	1	2					
Competitor 2		5	5	5	5	5	5	3	3					
Competitor 3		4	5	4	4	5	5	4	4					
CTQ Gap		-1	0	-1	-1	0	0	1	0					

FIGURE 12.16
Complete HOQ1 with roof and competitors.

12.3.4 How to Make Lemonade from Lemons

Consider the roof to be the source of product innovation. That roof pairs together all possible combinations of those CTQs. Some don't have interactions, and others have a negative or positive relationship. Those CTQ variables that exhibit a strongly negative interaction are the ones we need to pay attention to. When we pair these two strongly negative CTQs, we can potentially find an unanticipated product improvement. Let's look at a very common product first, and later, we can show you how it is applied to our existing HOQ.

We are all familiar with the ubiquitous writing instrument, the pencil. It has a sharp graphite tip allowing us to write or draw. The tip occasionally is sharpened to maintain the desired line thickness when writing.

Sometimes, we make mistakes and we need to eliminate the incorrect marks. At that moment, we revert to the anti-writing tool called the eraser. We pause, turn the pencil upside down to eliminate the mistake, brushing off with the back side of our hand the eraser scums, and we resume our stroke of genius.

The description of the pencil with an eraser shows how a single device can have a constructive part, the lead tip, and a destructive part the eraser. If we study this product, it is the combination of two components placed conveniently onto one product in opposite ends. The pencil can be all by itself, and the small handheld eraser as another item. Perhaps, for convenience of small mistakes that need to be erased, the built-in eraser on the pencil may be appropriate. However, if a larger amount of erasing is needed, the handheld eraser fits the job better.

The innovation of placing conveniently an eraser on a pencil happened many years ago. Nevertheless, it is important to learn how to think that two strongly negative CTQs can help inspire creativity on a product. Reverting back to Figure 12.16, where we have the completed roof, we can see three pairs of CTQs that have strongly negative (− −) symbols. Not all pairs of strongly negative interactions can lead to product innovation. Examining the relationship of **Cure Time** and **Sticky Tubes** could create a potential product improvement. Brainstorming ideas and concepts with the research team and members from other business functions can potentially break the strong negative relationship of time and tacky tubes by modifying the coatings formulation with other materials. Again, the whole point is to start a dialog about these strongly negative interactions and how a breakthrough solution can lead to product innovation.

Another method of using interactions to find groundbreaking solutions can be achieved by applying the principles of TRIZ (pronounced trees). TRIZ is the acronym from the following Russian words: Теория решения изобретательских задач (Teoriya resheniya izobretatel'skikh zadach) which translates to English as the Theory of Inventive Problem Solving. TRIZ makes use of the conflicting interactions especially of those that are strongly negative to find potential solutions to resolve that conflict.

The process involves two main steps. The first step matches the strong negative interaction from the roof with a pair of the 39 Contradictions that are already predefined in the Theory of Inventive Problem Solving. The second step places those Contradictions in a matrix to show how others have successfully solved these problems. The solutions fall under 40 Inventive Principles. The 39 Contradictions and 40 Inventive Principles have been researched and compiled by Genrich Altshuller. The source of the Contradictions and Inventive Principles came from patents. Altshuller carefully studied 40,000 patents to clearly understand the Contradictions, and it led to 39 distinct types. The Inventive Principle that each patent used to solve the issue was also categorized, and Altshuller detected 40 unique methods. This rich database of problems and solutions shows how issues were addressed in one industry under that patent. Altshuller helped interpret how it can be expanded into different industries which in turn can help your situation in a broader sense. This leap of using the solution from one trade to be applied onto another is a wonderful way of expanding the solution space. Also, at the same time, you are expanding the understanding of your problem in a broader and more holistic view to find a unique relationship of your roof interaction.

Here's an illustration that helps explain how the solution in a patent for a specific industry may transfer to solve the problem for another industry. When canning sweet peppers, the stalk and seeds must be removed. The removal process was done manually because automation couldn't handle the different pepper shapes and sizes. In 1968, the pepper canning method was granted a patent. The principle to remove the seeds was done by slowly pressurizing the peppers and quickly releasing the pressure. The sudden compression and expansion caused the joint of the stalk around the pepper to crack and pop out the seeds. The same agriculture application was able to shell sunflower seeds and shatter sugar crystals into powder. This application could also be applied outside the agriculture business.

In the diamond industry, the manufacturer cuts diamonds for shaping and final processing. The original method for shaping may cut through a fault, creating many small diamonds, becoming waste. These faults are hard to identify. By using the principles discovered from TRIZ, they were able to reduce the waste by pressurizing the diamonds, and immediately releasing the pressure to crack the diamonds at the fractures where the air was trapped. Using this new procedure, the diamond producer was able to shape the diamonds without cutting through the invisible fractures. This new application helped process diamonds with minimal waste.

If you would like to explore more about TRIZ, I would recommend two great sources. The first is a website pioneered by Ellen Dombs called triz-journal.com. Second is an informative book by John Terninko titled *Systematic Innovation: An Introduction to TRIZ (Theory of Inventive Problem Solving)*. Terninko's book is an excellent source to expand on this topic of innovation, and he truly outlines step by step to creative systematic innovation.

Using these methods can potentially expand your product offering. Again, as mentioned earlier, use the basement to know your competitive position and maintain it fresh with periodic updates from the field.

12.3.5 Four HOQs

So far, throughout this book, we used three HOQs. Under certain conditions, which we will examine shortly, we need to expand the three HOQs to four. Let's look at the audio system of a car. Because of the complexity of an audio system, four HOQs will be more beneficial, and we will show where this extra house fits.

We will start from the beginning with HOQ1. The VOC will capture the attributes that the customer will desire for an audio product, such as audio quality, satellite radio, AM/FM radio, and portable audio device connectivity. The CTQs define the metrics on how to deliver an audio product matching those VOC requirements. The combination of the two metrics fits nicely, as we did before, in HOQ1, the Customer House.

HOQ2 will relate those CTQs with Quality Control (QC) metrics defined by the research and development team. This house is the Translation house, converting the needs of the customer to QC metrics. These measurements can inform us ahead of time if we are delivering the desired product within customer specifications.

Now we introduce a different type of HOQ3, the Design House. This HOQ will combine the QC metrics that came from HOQ2 and relate to a new metric, the Design Variables (DVs). These DVs are internal or research-driven parameters that will go beyond any other metric that we saw in earlier HOQs. In fact, some of DVs can be considered leading indicators, providing an insight that is far more probing than the QCs or CTQs. Later, we will describe in more detail the DVs.

The fourth and last HOQ will combine the DVs with the Process Control metrics. When we had simpler products having three HOQs, we measured in production the QC variables to ensure that we matched customer specifications. Since we now introduced a more fundamental metric reading, the DVs, it can be used in production to predict QC values, becoming a leading metric. Let me provide an example of a DV that is considered a leading indicator. Bringing back the coating example for the brightly coated tubes, we in Liquid Paint Specialists make the paint used for the tubes. In Chapter 9, we related the QC metrics with the Process Variables. Also, we know based on the knowledge accumulated from the research and development team that the strong relationship of reactor temperature and orange peel appearance is well characterized. This association is fundamentally dependent on the rate of reaction which can be calculated with more data inputs from manufacturing and will be able to predict with good accuracy the level of orange peel. Using that DV will now anticipate ahead of time the QC metric. This is one step closer in doing statistical process control (SPC) by using rate of reaction instead of using orange peel which is statistical quality control (SQC). Many advanced companies prefer to identify the DVs that can be used as SPC instead of monitoring SQC. Again, as we stated previously, measuring something that is predictive is more advantageous, detecting the defect before it is shown as an out of specification CTQ. Also, it will minimize the amount of nonconformance product being made. As done already, this last house is called the Manufacturing house. Figure 12.17 shows all the four HOQs connected.

Sometimes, the explicit disclosure of the research-driven DVs may conflict with closely held trade secrets. For example, in the food or chemical industry, recipes contain explicitly all the ingredients and how to add properly each one and process each step. Here, you will need to use your judgment to ensure internal control mechanisms are applied to maintain security. Consider applying the HOQ concept that best fits your needs in the spirit of HOQ3, the Design House. By understanding the needs of your marketing contact from the commercial team (which came from HOQ2) and from your internal customer perhaps the engineer in manufacturing applying your specific DV to ensure manufacture ability of the product (which will impact HOQ4).

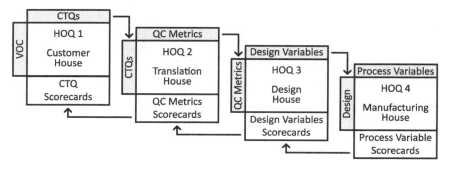

FIGURE 12.17
Four HOQs.

12.3.6 Conclusion

We have explored the use of the HOQ in many ways. We compressed from three HOQs to only one. Additionally, we reduced that single house to an HOQ flow down showing the list of metrics. Later, HOQ1 had new rooms added with competitive information. The VOC created the back porch and the CTQ made the new basement. The added rooms gave us perspectives of our product in the market against our competitors in a simple and quantifiable fashion. The CTQs became a focal point again. This time it was their interconnection, and how can the CTQ metrics positively or negatively impact each other. The results of those interactions were shown in the roof, a new section of HOQ1.

Lots of emphasis for last two techniques were described in HOQ1. However, it is important to note that the roof interactions and competitive analysis can be expanded to the other HOQs as well. Additionally, I have seen some practitioners use, in a novel way, the interactions on the VOC metrics. Since these variables do not cascade to another house, these don't become a roof of the next house, leaving those interactions unexamined.

We have outlined the best uses of the HOQs by actively listening to the customer. Only your imagination can limit the creative use and application of the HOQs.

13

Conclusion

13.1 THE LONG AND WINDING ROAD

You made it. You invested lots of time from your busy schedule to reach the last chapter of this book. You have acquired throughout these pages the process on how to make a better product to delight your customer. Perhaps you even jotted down some notes, and now you can see how your thinking has evolved. The new way of observing your customer through this lens creates a better focused product.

Back in Chapter 1, we explored the map to know what the journey will be and evaluated the possible routes that connect point A to B. We took time to study the trip. That same commitment of understanding the customer within a framework of the Houses of Quality (HOQs) helped us peer deeper into our product offering, market we serve, and companies we compete with. If you followed this book all along, you are now a stronger player in your field; you took the time to go slow to go fast. Consider yourself a strategist when you apply these tools.

To maintain this new way of defining your product, consider updating your HOQ annually. You may also update the Kano analysis and other tools at this time. Keep in mind that your viewpoint includes your customer, competitor, and the dynamics of the market. Perhaps, insert this exercise as part of your strategic plan. Prior to the strategic plan review, divide and conquer the components of all metrics by business functions, and as part of the strategic plan, review the data with all the business leaders. This will bring a new holistic, proactive view of the product in front of the entire business team.

13.1.1 Pontiac and Ice Cream

We have shared earlier that the customer speaks in the language of their industry, or if it is an end user, they may speak the experience they perceive. It is for these reasons, we have learned how to capture customer comments in HOQ1 and later place these in HOQ2, the Translation house.

The following example has made a strong impression on me, so much so, that I still remember the cold Michigan day back in March 2000. I received an email from our quality manager that epitomizes the importance of listening to the Voice of the Customer. Maybe the story is true or maybe it isn't, but the lesson learned was to take seriously what the customer described even if their terminology seemed unsophisticated. Here's the email I received:

A complaint was received by the Pontiac Division of General Motors:

> This is the second time I have written you, and I don't blame you for not answering me, because I kind of sounded crazy, but it is a fact that we have a tradition in our family of ice cream for dessert after dinner each night. But the kind of ice cream varies so, every night, after we've eaten, the whole family votes on which kind of ice cream we should have and I drive down to the store to get it. It's also a fact that I recently purchased a new Pontiac and since then my trips to the store have created a problem. You see, every time I buy vanilla ice cream, when I start back from the store my car won't start. If I get any other kind of ice cream, the car starts just fine. I want you to know I'm serious about this question, no matter how silly it sounds: 'What is there about a Pontiac that makes it not start when I get vanilla ice cream, and easy to start whenever I get any other kind?'

The Pontiac President was understandably skeptical about the letter but sent an engineer to check it out anyway. The latter was surprised to be greeted by a successful, obviously well-educated man in a fine neighborhood. He had arranged to meet the man just after dinner time, so the two hopped into the car and drove to the ice cream store. It was vanilla ice cream that night and, sure enough, after they came back to the car, it wouldn't start.

The engineer returned for three more nights. The first night, the man got chocolate. The car started. The second night, he got strawberry. The car started. The third night, he ordered vanilla. The car failed to start.

Now the engineer, being a logical man, refused to believe that this man's car was allergic to vanilla ice cream. He arranged, therefore, to continue his visits for as long as it took to solve the problem. And toward this end he began to take notes: he jotted down all sorts of data, time of day, type of gas used, time to drive back and forth, etc.

In a short time, he had a clue: the man took less time to buy vanilla than any other flavor. Why? The answer was in the layout of the store.

Vanilla, being the most popular flavor, was in a separate case at the front of the store for quick pick up. All the other flavors were kept in the back of the store at a different counter where it took considerably longer to find the flavor and get checked out.

Now the question for the engineer was why the car wouldn't start when it took less time. Once time became the problem—not the vanilla ice cream—the engineer quickly came up with the answer: vapor lock. It was happening every night, but the extra time taken to get the other flavors allowed the engine to cool down sufficiently to start. When the man got vanilla, the engine was still too hot for the vapor lock to dissipate.

Moral of the story: even insane-looking problems are sometimes real.

I included this story because it took time to understand the problem. It took time to go slow to go fast. I was also informed that this event triggered a recall to fix the affected Pontiac vehicles, and they were reconfigured to minimize the vapor lock issue which prevented the engine from starting. Again, fact or fiction, it is a great story to put in perspective that customers may not speak the language as eloquently as the supplier may want.

13.1.2 A Parting Thought

A police officer (now turned deacon) once said, when you have facts, you have true statements. It reflects that reality. When you combine facts, now you have a story. Using that thinking on our situation, when you have metrics, you have true values of the property. Now combining several properties and functionalities, you have a unique product. We showed how the Voice of the Customer gave us the facts we needed to modify throughout our organization. That is what we have done throughout this book: hearing the Voice of the Customer on the factory floor.

Enjoy the journey!

References

Cafaro, Paul G. 2017a. Threading the voice of the customer to the factory floor: A novel approach of using DFSS and CI tools to connect customer expectations to process capabilities. In *IMPACT Manufacturing Summit*, Schaumburg, IL, 2017, 1–15. Hermosa Beach, CA: Quartz Events.

Cafaro, Paul G. 2017b. Threading the voice of the customer to the factory floor: A novel approach combining design for Six Sigma and continuous improvement tools. In *AME Boston 2017 Conference*, Boston, MA, 2017, 1–15. Rolling Meadows, IL: Association for Manufacturing Excellence.

Covey, Stephen R. 1989. *The Seven Habits of Highly Effective People: Restoring the Character Ethic*. New York: Simon & Schuster.

Hart, David, and Paul G. Cafaro. 2016. Building a balanced productivity performance plan. In *IMPACT Manufacturing Summit*, Schaumburg, IL, 2016, 11–21. Hermosa Beach, CA: Quartz Events.

Terninko, John, Alla Zusman, and Boris Zlotin. 1998. *Systematic Innovation: An Introduction to TRIZ (Theory of Inventive Problem Solving)*. Boca Raton, FL: St. Lucie Press.

TRIZ Journal. 2019. *The TRIZ Journal*. https://triz-journal.com.

Ziglar, Zig. 2003. *Selling 101: What Every Successful Sales Professional Needs to Know*. Nashville, TN: Thomas Nelson Publishers.

Index

A

Anti-writing tool, 126

B

Basic Needs, Kano model, 17–19, 22, 23,
  25, 28, 36–38
Brainstorming
  attributes, 12–15
  open-ended questions, 33
  process variables, 76
  session with company employees, 24, 28

C

Cage of safety, 115
Car subsystems, Houses of Quality,
  115–116
Certificate of analysis (COA), 28
Closed-ended Kano questions
  customers
    responses, 36, 37
    visits, 28–29
  ratings summary, 39
COA, see Certificate of analysis (COA)
Coating technologies
  of polyurethane resin, 112
  of wood application, 112–113
Commercial function, 6, 7, 119
Competitors, 117–121
Complexity
  less complex product, see Less complex
    product, Houses of Quality
  moderately complex product,
    see Moderately complex
    product, Houses of Quality
  complex product, see Moderately
    complex product, Houses of
    Quality
Complex products
  Houses of Quality

design variables, 128–129
lemonade from lemons, making,
  125–128
roof of HOQ1, 121–125
subsystems, 114–116
VOCs and CTQs with competitors,
  117–121
Conduct interview
  voice of the customer, 34
    closed-ended Kano questions, 36,
      37, 39
    open-ended questions, 34–36, 38
Consumer Reports, 42
Control Plan
  customer/production specifications,
    90–91
  definition of, 87–88
  parts of, 88
  process variables, 88, 89
  reaction plan, 88–90
  revisions and training, 91
Crack rates
  critical to quality, 50, 52, 55
  house of quality 1, 62
  standard operating procedure, 42
Critical to quality (CTQs) metrics
  customer metrics, 43–46
  Houses of Quality
    competitors, 117–121
    manufacturing scorecard
      metrics, 101
  industry, 41–43
  organizing, 46–47
  and quality control metrics, 67–69
  translation house, 46, 47
    combined, 50–56
    organizing, 49–50
  for Tubing Experts, 47
CTQ metrics, see Critical to quality
  (CTQ) metrics
Cured film build, 44, 46
Cure time, 42, 123, 126